A Manual for Writers

A Manual for Writers
of Term Papers, Theses,
and Dissertations

Fourth Edition

Kate L. Turabian

The University of Chicago Press

Chicago and London

The University of Chicago Press, Chicago 60637
The University of Chicago Press, Ltd., London

Fourth Edition, published 1973

Printed in the United States of America

ISBN: 0–226–81620–6 (clothbound); 0–226–81621–4 (paperbound)
Library of Congress Catalog Card Number: 73–77792
77   76
10 9 8 7 6

Contents

Preface

This *Manual for Writers of Term Papers, Theses, and Dissertations* is designed as a guide to suitable style in the typewritten presentation of formal papers both in scientific and in nonscientific fields. While the ideas, the findings, and the conclusions put forth in the paper are of primary importance, their consideration by the reader depends in considerable measure upon an orderly presentation, well documented and free of mechanical flaws.

The genesis of this "thesis manual" lies in a sentence of the June 1929 edition of the *Handbook of the Graduate Schools* of the University of Chicago, which read: "Samples of paper and directions concerning the form of the dissertation may be obtained at the Dissertation Desk, in Harper Library." When in 1931 the work of the Dissertation Desk was transferred to a dissertation secretary under the purview of the Dean of Students, the secretary inherited a one-page set of mimeographed instructions, the first paragraph stating, "In form, the dissertation should follow the style of the University of Chicago Press as exhibited in its publications and set forth in *A Manual of Style*." Students and their typists, therefore, were directed to that style manual for necessary detailed information concerning acceptable thesis form. But the *Manual of Style*, designed as a guide to typographers, editors, advertising writers, and others dealing with the printed word, required some interpretation if it was to serve as a guide to a person who was to produce a typescript conforming to its dictates. To supplement the Press *Manual*, the dissertation secretary furnished to students a two-page set of mimeographed instructions on such matters as spacing, indention, margins, underlining. With the flattening of student pocketbooks in the depression of 1930–35, there appeared to be a need to expand those instructions into a small booklet which would incorporate the materials in *A Manual of*

Style that were relevant to the preparation of a typewritten dissertation. The title of the booklet was essentially the same that it bears today. Thus from the beginning the thesis manual has recommended in general the style of the University of Chicago Press as shown in its publications — both books and journals — and as explained in its *Manual of Style.*

The publication of the twelfth edition of the Press *Manual* in 1969 represented the first revision of that work since 1949, reflecting thus a twenty-year change in the reporting of scholarly and scientific investigation — a change that has moved increasingly toward simplification in literary style. That edition of *A Manual of Style* and my desire to pass along to students information on changes of style that afford economies in time and money have led to the preparation of this fourth edition of *A Manual for Writers of Term Papers, Theses, and Dissertations.*

Certain Latin abbreviations long familiar in footnote citations are eliminated in favor of the more readily identifiable short-form titles in secondary references. Other Latin abbreviations still in use are no longer underlined. The section on punctuation (now in chap. 3) is expanded, and there is further clarification in the employment of ellipsis points and in the expression of numbers. Finally, the use of arabic instead of roman numerals is recommended in *references* to the several parts of published works. Here it may be pointed out that the change to arabic numerals in references does not imply disapproval of capital roman numerals to express chapter or part numbers as they may appear at the heads of chapters or on part-title pages of a paper or dissertation. Special care has been given to the selection of examples, and there are more of them than in earlier editions.

It is not within the scope of this thesis manual to give instruction in English composition. The assumption is that if the student feels the need of further training in this field, he will consult an up-to-date work such as the excellent, widely used book on expository writing by Porter G. Perrin, *Writer's Guide and Index to English,* 5th edition (Glenview, Ill.: Scott, Foresman & Co., 1972).

In the natural sciences, where there is considerable variation in the methods of making reference to works in the several fields, students might profit from consulting the particular style manual or guide prepared by the outstanding scholarly association in his field. The following publications may be found in all college and university libraries and in most public libraries, and they may be procured from the publishers in each case. American Institute of Physics, *Style Manual for Guidance in the Preparation of Papers,* 2d revised edition (New York: American Institute of Physics, 1967). American Mathematical Society, "Manual for Authors of Mathematical Papers," reprinted from *Bulletin of the American Mathematical Society,* vol. 68, no. 5 (September 1962). Council of Biology Editors, Committee on Form and Style, *CBE Style Manual,* 3d edition (Washington, D.C.: American Institute of Biological Sciences, 1972). American Psychological Association, *Publication Manual,* 1967 revision (Washington, D.C.: American Psychological Association, 1967). The writer who is preparing a work for publication will find much helpful information in the twelfth edition of *A Manual of Style* (Chicago: University of Chicago Press, 1969).

I am greatly indebted to the University of Chicago Press for its generous cooperation in making this publication possible. In all my association with the Press, its directors and numerous staff members, past and present, have given me warm encouragement and shown me much kindness, besides teaching me a good part of what I know about bibliographical style.

1   The Parts of the Paper

1:1   A paper[1] is normally made up of three main parts: the front matter, or preliminaries, the text, and the reference matter. In a long paper each of these main parts may consist of several sections (see below); but in a short paper there may be nothing more than a title page and text, the latter with or without subheadings, tables, illustrations, as the topic and treatment may require. The inclusion of a table or two, an illustration or two, does not automatically call for a list of tables and a list of illustrations; and for some papers a table of contents may have little value. These are matters, however, that must be left to the good sense of the writer, who should know best what arrangements are suitable for his particular piece of work.

1:2   The *order* of the following outline, regardless of the parts that may be omitted, should be observed. (Note that a table of contents and a list of illustrations or tables come before the preface. This is a change from the order specified in the third edition of this *Manual*.)

The front matter, or *preliminaries*:

Frontispiece (see par. 11:4)

Title page

Blank page

Table of contents

List of illustrations

List of tables

---

[1]The term "paper" is used throughout this *Manual* to refer alike to term papers, reports, theses, and dissertations except in matters relating specifically to one of them.

Preface, including acknowledgments, or acknowledgments alone unless these appear as the final paragraph in the paper

The text:

Introduction

Main body of the paper, usually consisting of well-defined divisions, such as parts, chapters, sections, etc., and including footnotes

The reference matter:

Appendix(es)

Bibliography

Additional reference material, such as a glossary or a list of abbreviations devised specifically for use in the paper

THE FRONT MATTER, OR PRELIMINARIES

TITLE PAGE

1:3   Most universities and colleges have their own style of title page for theses and dissertations, and this should be followed exactly in matters of content and spacing. For term papers and reports, if a sample sheet is not provided, a title page might logically include the name of the university or college (usually centered at the top of the sheet), the exact title of the paper, the course, the date, and the name of the writer—all suitably capitalized, centered, and spaced upon the page.

TABLE OF CONTENTS

1:4   The table of contents, sometimes headed simply "Contents," includes the list of illustrations, list of tables, preface (or acknowledgments), introduction, chapters (or their equivalents) with their numbers and titles, appendix(es), and bibliography, with the page numbers of each. If the chapters are grouped under "parts," the numbers and titles (if any) of the parts also appear in the contents. Subheadings within the chapters are frequently included, in one of various ways, or they may be omitted entirely from the table of contents. Four styles of tables of contents are shown in samples A–D following this chapter. (Note that none of these samples gives the complete contents of a paper. For suggestions on spacing and other matters related to typing the table of contents, see pars. 13:14–16.)

1:5   In preparing a table of contents for a paper containing subheadings of one or more levels (see par. 1:18), there is great latitude in choosing both the amount of information included and the method of presenting it. At one extreme, the contents may provide what is essentially an outline by including all the levels (sample B). At the other extreme, the contents may omit the subheadings — even though the paper may carry subheadings of one level or more than one — showing only the chapter numbers and titles. For many papers, both those with only one level and those with more than one level of subheadings, the contents includes the first-level (principal) subheadings, with or without the page numbers (sample A). Note that when more than one level of subheading is included in the contents, each must appear in order of its rank; that is, it is not permissible to begin with any but the first-level, or to skip from the first- to the third- or fourth-level.

THE UNIVERSITY OF CHICAGO

INTERNAL RELATEDNESS AND PLURALISM IN THE
PHILOSOPHY OF WHITEHEAD

A DISSERTATION SUBMITTED TO
THE FACULTY OF THE DIVISION OF THE HUMANITIES
IN CANDIDACY FOR THE DEGREE OF
DOCTOR OF PHILOSOPHY

DEPARTMENT OF PHILOSOPHY

BY
WILLIAM PAINE ALSTON

CHICAGO, ILLINOIS
MARCH 1951

Example of title page for a dissertation

1:6   As for the method of including subheadings in the contents, if more than one level is shown, each level is indented three spaces below the preceding higher level (sample B). If only the first-level is shown, each subheading may be indented three spaces below the chapter title (sample A), or, if the subheadings are short, the first one in each chapter is indented three spaces below the chapter title and the following ones are run in (samples C and D). Punctuation separating run-in subheadings may be semicolons, dashes, or periods. (For page numbers with subheadings, see par. 1:10.)

1:7   The wording of part and chapter titles and of all subheadings should follow exactly their wording within the body of the paper, although the capitalization of subheadings, as indicated below (par. 1:8), may differ from that appearing in the text.

1:8   *Capitalization* of titles in the table of contents should be as follows: For the titles of all major divisions (contents, list of illustrations, list of tables, preface, introduction, parts, chapters, appendix, bibliography), capitalize all letters (e.g., PREFACE). Subheadings may be capitalized in one of two ways: (1) capitalize the initial letter of the first and last words and of all words except articles, prepositions, and coordinate conjunctions (sample D); or (2) capitalize only the initial letter of the first subheading under the chapter and of proper nouns and proper adjectives (sample C).

1:9   *Numbers* designating parts and chapters should be given as they are in the text. Part numbers may be capital roman numerals (PART I, PART II, etc.) or spelled-out numbers (PART ONE, PART TWO, etc.). The number may precede the part title and be separated from it by a period (sample A) or it may be centered above the title and thus need no punctuation (sample C). Chapter numbers may be arabic or capital roman numerals or spelled-out numbers. The word "Chapter" is sometimes included with the number (sample D) or is placed over all the chapter numbers (samples A and B) or it may be omitted (sample C). Do not use the word "Chapter" in the contents if the sections of the paper are not so designated.

1:10   *Page numbers* in a typed table of contents are always given at the right-hand side of the page, each following a line of dots (period leaders) from the title of the section. Note that only the *beginning* page number of each chapter or other section is given. Page numbers for parts may be omitted unless they are not evidenced by the beginning page number of the first chapter under each part. Note that if the page number is given for one part, it must be given for all of them. Page numbers for subheadings may also be omitted; when they are included with run-in subheadings, they are best placed within parentheses immediately following the subheadings (sample D). (For alignment of leaders and page numbers, see par. 13:14.)

LIST OF ILLUSTRATIONS

1:11   A list of illustrations, sometimes headed simply "Illustrations," consists of the figure numbers (indicated with arabic numerals), the legends (titles) of all the figures, and the page numbers. The legends should agree with those given under the illustrations, although if they are long, it is usually permissible to give them in shortened form in the list. For a thesis or dissertation, however, checking with the dissertations department is advisable. But if a descriptive or explanatory statement appears in addition to the legend under the illustration, there should be no hesitancy about omitting such a statement in the list of illustrations. (See sample E.)

1:12   In the list of illustrations, *but not under the illustrations* (par. 11:8), the legends are typed in capital and small letters (i.e., capitalize the initial letter of the first and last words and all words except articles, prepositions, and coordinate conjunctions). If in addition to illustrations called figures, there are others designated specifically as maps or charts or graphs (e.g., Map 1), these should be included in the list of illustrations, in separate sections under their designated labels (see sample F).

LIST OF TABLES

1:13   A list of tables gives the table numbers with their respective titles and page numbers. The titles as shown in the list should agree exactly with their wording above the tables themselves. Table numbers are expressed in arabic numerals, and the titles are typed in capital and small letters, as for legends in the list of illustrations (see par. 1:12 and sample G).

PREFACE (OR ACKNOWLEDGMENTS)

1:14 Included in the preface are such matters as the writer's reasons for making the study, its background, scope, and purpose, and acknowledgment of the aids afforded him in the process of the research and writing by institutions and persons. If the writer thinks he has nothing significant to say about the study that is not covered in the main body of the paper and wishes only to acknowledge the various sorts of assistance that he has received, he should entitle his remarks "Acknowledgments" rather than "Preface."[2]

THE TEXT

INTRODUCTION

1:15 The text ordinarily begins with an introduction, which may be chapter 1. If it is short, the writer may prefer to head it simply "Introduction" and reserve the more formal heading "Chapter" for the longer sections of which the main body of the paper is composed. But the introduction, whether it is called chapter 1 or not, is the first major division of the text, not the last of the preliminaries, as is sometimes supposed. Thus the first page of the introduction is page 1 (arabic numeral) of the paper.

CHAPTERS OR THEIR EQUIVALENTS

1:16 The main body of the paper is usually divided into chapters, each chapter having a title and each beginning on a new page. In a short paper some writers prefer to omit the

[2]Although the student would wish to acknowledge special assistance such as consultation on technical matters and aid in securing special equipment and source materials, he may with propriety omit an expression of formal thanks for the routine help given by an adviser or a thesis committee.

word "Chapter" and to use merely numerals—roman or arabic—in sequence before the headings of the several main divisions. In a long paper some writers like to group related chapters into "parts," with or without individual titles (see sample A, p. 11). In that case, each part is preceded by a part-title page.

PART-TITLE PAGES

1:17   Part-title pages (sometimes referred to as half-title pages) are required if the chapters are grouped under "parts," the part-title page being placed immediately before the first chapter of the group composing the part. Since the introduction is to the *entire* paper, whether or not it is titled "Chapter 1," it is not included in "Part I." The first part-title page therefore follows rather than precedes the introduction.

SUBHEADINGS

1:18   In some papers the chapters or their equivalents are divided into sections, which may in turn be divided into subsections, and these into sub-subsections, and so on. Such divisions are customarily given titles, called *subheadings,* which are designated respectively *first-, second-,* and *third-level* subheadings and differentiated from one another by typing style. The style of subheading with the greatest attention value should be given to the principal, or first-level, subdivision. On a typewritten page centered headings have greater attention value than side headings, and underlined headings, centered or side, have greater attention value than those not underlined. A plan for the display of five levels of subheadings in a typed paper follows:

First-level, centered heading, underlined:

Traditional Controversy between Medieval
Church and State

Second-level, centered heading, not underlined:

Reappearance of Religious Legalism

Third-level, side heading underlined, beginning at the left margin:

Jesus and Paul

Fourth-level, side heading, not underlined:

The Gospel as initiated
by Jesus

Fifth-level, heading run into (at the beginning of) a paragraph and underlined:

The gospel legalized in the Church. The gospel
that was offered by the early Christians to the pagans
. . . was made available through the Church.

Note that first- and second-level subheadings are typed in capital and small letters (i.e., first and last words and all other words except articles, prepositions, and coordinate conjunctions capitalized), and that lower-level subheadings capitalize only the first word, proper nouns, and proper adjectives.

1:19 If fewer than five levels are required, they may be selected in any suitable *descending order,* as indicated above. (For spacing subheadings see pars. 13:24–25.)

FOOTNOTES

1:20 Footnotes, also considered part of the text, are discussed in chapter 6.

THE REFERENCE MATTER

APPENDIX

1:21 An appendix, although by no means an essential part of every paper, is a useful device to make available to the reader material related to the text but not suitable for inclusion in it. Such material may be tables too detailed for text presentation; technical notes on method, and schedules and forms used in collecting materials; copies of documents not generally available to the reader; case studies too long to be put into the text; and sometimes figures or other illustrative materials.

1:22   If the materials relegated to an appendix are numerous and fall into several categories, each category should form a separate appendix. Where there is more than one appendix, each should be given a number or a letter (Appendix 1, Appendix 2, etc.; or, Appendix A, Appendix B, etc.).

1:23   The writer may use his discretion about whether a single appendix should carry a title, like a chapter title. If there is more than one appendix, however, each should carry a descriptive title.

1:24   Whether to type an appendix in single or double space depends upon the nature of the material; spacing need not be the same for all the appendixes. Documents and case studies may well be in single space, whereas explanations of methods and procedures may be in double space, like the text, for instance.

GLOSSARY

1:25   If a paper contains many foreign words or technical words and phrases not likely to be familiar to the reader, a list of these words, with their translations or definitions, will be helpful. The words should be arranged in alphabetical order, like a dictionary. Each word should be typed flush with the left margin and followed by a comma or a colon and the translation or definition. Any runover lines should be indented three spaces. If any of the definitions consist of one or more sentences, all entries should end with a period. If all definitions consist only of words or phrases, no final punctuation should be used. Double space should appear between items.

LIST OF ABBREVIATIONS

1:26   A list of abbreviations at the end of a paper is desirable only if the author has used a number of arbitrarily devised abbreviations in his footnotes, or elsewhere. It is not necessary to list commonly accepted abbreviations, such as those used for the titles of journals in various fields. Any such list should, like a glossary, be arranged in alphabetical order — by the abbreviation itself, not its spelled-out form. The punctuation and typing style of the list should be the same as that recommended for a glossary (par. 1:25).

BIBLIOGRAPHY

1:27   The bibliography is the last section of the paper (except in those rare instances where a paper carries an index, like a book). Instructions for the preparation and style of a bibliography are set forth in chapters 7 and 8.

SAMPLE A. Partial table of contents for a work in which chapters are grouped under "parts." First-level subheadings only are shown and their individual page numbers are omitted. (See par. 1:5.)

TABLE OF CONTENTS

SAMPLE B. Partial table of contents showing three levels of subheadings with page numbers. Note that runover lines in subheadings are indented to the third space.

SAMPLE C. Partial table of contents in which only first-level subheadings are shown, run in under chapter headings, and individual page numbers omitted.

CONTENTS

SAMPLE D. Partial table of contents in which first-level subheadings, each with its beginning page number, are run in under chapter headings.

CONTENTS

SAMPLE E. List of illustrations all of which are the same type.

SAMPLE F. List of illustrations in which two types are shown.

SAMPLE G. List of tables, showing the number of the table, the title, and the page number.

LIST OF TABLES

2 Abbreviations and Numbers

ABBREVIATIONS

2:1 Abbreviations *in text,* except in scientific and technical writing, have long been frowned upon. In footnotes and bibliographies, in tabular matter, and in some kinds of illustrations (e.g., maps, graphs, charts), however, abbreviations not only are permitted but are normally preferred. Also, there are a few words that are almost never spelled out. (How many, I wonder, know the word for which *Mrs.* is the abbreviation?)

WITH PERSONAL NAMES

2:2 Use the following abbreviations for social titles before names: Mr., Messrs., Mrs., Mlle, M., MM., Mme, Sr., and corresponding abbreviations in other foreign languages (note that after Mlle and Mme there is no period).

2:3 Use the abbreviation Dr. before a name, but spell out the word *doctor* when it appears without a name:

Dr. Bixby came at once.
The doctor was out of town.

2:4 Use abbreviations for scholastic degrees and professional affiliations after names: M.A., Ph.D., Litt.D., M.D., F.R.S., and so on. A comma precedes such an abbreviation when it follows a name:

Thomas Q. Donne, Ph.D.

2:5 Use the abbreviations Sr., Jr., II, III (for Senior, Junior, Second, Third) following a full name. Never use the spelled-out words or the abbreviations with the surname alone. (In informal writing it is permissible to use the terms

16

with given names.) Note that a comma precedes Jr. and Sr., but not II, III:

```
Christopher Morley, Jr.   Mrs. Joseph P. Turner, Sr.
But:   Adlai E. Stevenson III
```

2:6   Spell out a civil, military, professional, or religious title when it precedes the surname alone:

```
Senator Fulbright   Governor Rockefeller
Professor Gale   General Fairweather   Father Kennedy
```

But use the appropriate abbreviation before a full name:

```
Sen. J. William Fulbright   Gov. Nelson A. Rockefeller
Brig. Gen. Thomas Fairweather   Prof. Gordon Gale
```

2:7   Spell out *Reverend* and *Honorable* if preceded by *the*; otherwise abbreviate to Rev. and Hon. Never use the title, either spelled out or abbreviated, with the surname alone, but only when it is followed by the person's full name, or by Mr. or Dr. as may be appropriate:

```
Wrong:   Rev. Bentley (or the Rev. Bentley)
Right:   Rev. John Bentley (or the Reverend John
         Bentley, or the Reverend Dr. Bentley, or
         Rev. Dr. Bentley)
```

2:8   *Saint* standing before the name of a saint may be abbreviated, St. (plural, SS.):

```
St. Thomas Aquinas   SS. Augustine and Benedict
```

2:9   Names preceded by *Saint* are spelled out or abbreviated, as personal preference on the part of the bearers of such names may determine:

```
Etienne Geoffroy Saint-Hilaire
Louis Stephen St. Laurent
```

BOOKS OF THE BIBLE

2:10   Spell out the names of the books of the Bible and of the Apocrypha, except when they occur with exact references.

2:11   Acceptable abbreviations may be found in the front matter of the Bible, in the *Shorter Oxford English Dictionary*,

17

and in the University of Chicago Press *Manual of Style.*
Place a colon between chapter and verse number(s).

Some Bible scholars do not believe that the Gospel
of John was written by the Apostle John.

The Beatitudes are found in Matt. 5:3–12.

GEOGRAPHIC NAMES

2:12   Spell out the names of countries (except that USSR is
now commonly used for Union of Socialist Soviet Re-
publics), states, counties, provinces, territories, bodies of
water, mountains, and the like.

2:13   Spell out the prefixes of geographic names: Fort, Lake,
Mount, Point, Port, Saint:

Mount Prospect   Saint Louis

2:14   Spell out all such words as *avenue, street, drive, road,
court, square, terrace, building,* capitalizing only when
they are used as part of a name:

Many faculty members live in Bryant Terrace.

Charming Georgian houses stand in the old square.

2:15   Spell out *north, south, east, west,* as well as *northeast,
southwest,* and so on, capitalizing when they are part of
a name, and abbreviating when they follow a street name:

The seminary is in West Newton, Massachusetts.

The shop is at 245 Seventeenth Street NW.

High-rise apartments are going up on the northwest
side of the city.

TIME

2:16   Spell out the names of months and of days when they occur
in text, whether alone or in dates. But in footnotes, bibliographies, tables (and other closely set matter), the following designations are permissible if used consistently:
Jan., Feb., Mar., Apr., May, June, July, Aug., Sept., Oct.,
Nov., Dec.; Sun., Mon., Tues., Wed., Thurs., Fri., Sat.

2:17   Use the abbreviations A.M., P.M., and M. after numerals
indicating time of day. Note that the abbreviation for noon
is M.; that for midnight is P.M. (see par. 2:42).

2:18   For era designations use the abbreviations B.C., A.D., B.C.E., or C.E. ("before Christ," "anno Domini," "before the common era," "common era"). A.D. should precede the year number, and the other designations should follow it:

> Solomon's Temple was destroyed by the Babylonians in 587 B.C. Rebuilt in 515 B.C., it was destroyed by the Romans in A.D. 70.

MEASUREMENTS

2:19   Spell out expressions of dimension, distance, measure, weight, degree, and so on (but see par. 2:50).

PARTS OF A BOOK

2:20   Spell out the words *book, chapter, part, volume, section, scene, verse, column, page, figure, plate,* and so on, except that when such a term is followed by a number in footnote and parenthetical material, abbreviation is preferred: bk(s)., chap(s)., pt(s)., vol(s)., sec(s)., sc., v. (vv.), col(s)., p. (pp.), fig(s)., pl(s). The words *act, line,* and *table* should never be abbreviated.

ORGANIZATIONS

2:21   It is now general practice to refer to many government agencies, unions, service and fraternal organizations, network broadcasting companies, and so on, by the initials of their names, omitting periods. For unfamiliar abbreviations, the name should be spelled out at its first occurrence and the abbreviation placed in parentheses immediately after. Following are some of the better-known abbreviations:

AMA	AFL–CIO	IOOF	CORE
NATO	NBC	YMCA	CIA
UNESCO	UN	YMHA	HEW

2:22   Some abbreviations should be used in giving the names of companies, even though the individual firm name does not abbreviate the word: &, Bro., Bros., Co., Corp. *The* before a name, and *Inc.* or *Ltd.* following it, are usually omitted; when *the* is needed in the context, it is not treated as part of the title and therefore is not capitalized:

19

```
The book was published by the University of
Chicago Press.
```

NUMBERS

GENERAL RULE

2:23   In scientific material all measurements are expressed in figures (par. 2:49). In nonscientific material numbers are sometimes spelled out and sometimes expressed in figures, according to prescribed rules. The general rule followed by many writers and by the University of Chicago Press, is to spell out all numbers up through one hundred — e.g., sixty-five, ninety-eight — and all round numbers that can be expressed in two words — e.g., one hundred, two hundred, five thousand, forty-five hundred:

```
At that time the population of Israel was less than
three million.
```

Exact numbers over one hundred are written as figures:

```
There are 514 seniors in the graduating class.
```

SERIES

2:24   The general rule requires modification when numbers above *and* below one hundred appear in a series, or group, of numbers each of which applies to the same kind of thing. Here all are expressed in figures:

```
In the area studied, there were 186 such buildings,
the smaller housing anywhere from 50 to 65 persons
each, and the larger from 650 to 900 each, with a
single room sometimes occupied by 8 to 10.
```

INITIAL NUMBERS

2:25   A sentence should never begin with a figure, even when there are figures in the rest of the sentence. Either spell out the first number or, better, recast the sentence:

```
Two hundred and fifty passengers escaped injury;
175 sustained minor injuries; 110 were so seriously
hurt that they required hospitalization.
```

20

Or, better:
There were 250 passengers who escaped injury;
175 who sustained minor injuries; and 110 who were
so seriously hurt that they required hospitalization.

ROUND NUMBERS

2:26   Although round numbers occurring in isolation are spelled
out (par. 2:23), several round numbers occurring close
together are usually expressed in figures:

There were 1,500 books in the first shipment, 8,000
in the second, and 100,000 in the third; altogether
there were now about 1,000,000 volumes in the ware-
house.

2:27   Very large round numbers are frequently expressed in
figures and units of millions or billions:

This means that Japan will require about 7.8 million
barrels of oil a day compared with 3.2 million
barrels a day in current consumption.

PERCENTAGES AND DECIMALS

2:28   Figures should be used to express decimals and percentages. The word *percent* should be written out, except in
scientific writing, where the symbol % may be used:

With interest at 8 percent, the monthly payment
would amount to $12.88, which he noted was exactly
2.425 times the amount he was accustomed to save
monthly.

FRACTIONS

2:29   A fraction standing alone should be spelled out, but a
numerical unit composed of a whole number and a fraction
should be expressed in figures:

Trade and commodity services accounted for nine-
tenths of all international receipts and payments.
Cabinets with $10\frac{1}{2}$-by-$32\frac{1}{4}$-inch shelves were installed.

MONEY

2:30   *United States currency.* The general rule (par. 2:23) applies in isolated references to amounts of money in United
States currency. If the amount is spelled out, so are the
words *dollars* and *cents*; if figures are used, the dollar symbol ($) precedes them:

Rarely do they spend more than five dollars a week
on recreation.

But:
The report showed $135 collected in fines.

Fractional amounts of money over one dollar appear in
figures like other decimal fractions ($1.75). When both
fractional amounts and whole-dollar amounts are used in
the same sentence (and only in such circumstances), the
whole-dollar amounts are shown with a decimal point and
ciphers:

The same article is sold by some stores for $1.75,
by others for $1.95, and by still others for $2.00.

2:31   The expression of very large amounts of money, which
may be cumbersome whether spelled out in full or written
in figures, may well follow the rule for expressing large
round numbers (par. 2:27), using units of millions or billions with figures preceded by the dollar sign:

Japan's exports to Taiwan, which averaged $60 million
between 1954 and 1958, rose sharply to $210 million
in 1965, and $250 million in 1966.

The deficit that year was $10.4 billion.

2:32   *British currency.* Since decimalization went into effect in
February 1971, British currency has been expressed in
pounds and pence, very like dollars and cents:

two pounds   twenty-five pence
£3.50   25 p.

Before decimalization, British currency was expressed in
pounds, shillings, and pence:

threepence   seventeen shillings   four pounds
two shillings and sixpence
£12 17s. 6d.   or   £12.17.6   £48 million

£1,238 million

22

A sum of money might also be expressed in *guineas* (twenty-one shillings equaled a guinea):

```
thirty guineas (gns.)    342 guineas
```

The term *billion* should not be used for British sums, since *billion* as employed by the British means *trillion* in United States terminology.

2:33 *Other foreign currencies.* Most foreign currencies follow a system like that of the United States, employing unit symbols before the figures. They do vary, however, in their expressions of large numbers and decimals. The student whose paper must deal with sums of money in currencies other than United States or British is advised to consult the table "Foreign Money" in the United States Government Printing Office *Style Manual*.

PARTS OF WRITTEN WORKS

2:34 With few exceptions, all the numbered parts of printed works are cited in arabic numerals. If, however, a reference is made to the preliminary pages of a work that designates those pages with small roman numerals, the reference should also employ that style.

2:35 Citations to public documents or other manuscript material should use exactly the kind of numerals found in the source.

DATES

2:36 *Day, month, and year.* One of the two permissible styles for expressing day, month, and year should be followed consistently throughout the paper. The first, in which punctuation is omitted, is preferred:

```
On 28 June 1970 the Convocation Pacem in Maribus
was convened.

Or:
On June 28, 1970, the Convocation Pacem in Maribus
was convened.
```

2:37 When the day, month, and year are mentioned as in the foregoing examples, note that *st, d,* or *th* does not appear after the day. But when the day alone is given, or when the day is separated from the month by one or more words, the preferred style is to spell out the day of the month:

```
The date set was the twenty-ninth.
The sequence of events of the tenth of June is
unclear.
Or:
The sequence of events of 10 June is unclear.
```

2:38   When month and year alone are mentioned, the preferred style is to omit punctuation between them: June 1970.

2:39   In informal writing it is permissible to abbreviate reference to the year:

```
It would certainly appear that the November '70
election did not strengthen the Republican position.
```

2:40   *Centuries.* References to particular centuries should be spelled out, uncapitalized:

```
the eighteenth century   the mid-twentieth century
seventeenth-century literature
```

2:41   *Decades.* References to decades take two forms. The context sometimes determines the one chosen:

```
The 1890s saw an enormous increase in the use of
manufactured gas.
During the thirties traffic decreased by 50 percent.
```

TIME OF DAY

2:42   Except when A.M. or P.M. is used, time of day should be spelled out in text matter. Never add *in the morning* after A.M. or *in the evening* after P.M., and never use *o'clock* with either A.M. or P.M. or with figures. Write, for example:

```
The train was due to arrive at 7:10 A.M.
The meeting was called for 8:00 P.M.
Or:
The meeting was called for eight o'clock in the
evening.
```

Where the context makes clear whether it is morning or evening that is meant, you might write simply:

```
The meeting was called for eight o'clock.
The night operator takes calls from eleven to seven.
```

Midnight is written as 12:00 P.M., noon as 12:00 M.

NUMBERS WITH NAMES

2:43 *Rulers.* In a succession of emperors, kings, queens, or popes with the same name, identification is by numerals, traditionally capital roman:

```
Charles V        Henry VIII      Elizabeth II
Napoleon III     Louis XIV       John XXIII
```

2:44 *Family names.* Male members of families with identical names are sometimes differentiated in the same way as monarchs:

```
Adlai E. Stevenson III
```

See also paragraph 2:5.

2:45 *Governmental designations.* Particular dynasties, governments, governing bodies, political divisions, and military subdivisions are commonly designated by an ordinal number before the noun and are capitalized. Numerals of less than one hundred should be spelled out; those over one hundred, written in figures:

```
Nineteenth Dynasty      Eighty-first Congress
Fifth Republic          First Continental Congress
Third Reich             Twenty-fourth Congressional
Sixth Ward              District
But:  173d Airborne Division
```

2:46 *Churches, lodges, unions.* Numerals standing before the names of churches or religious organizations are usually spelled-out ordinals:

```
Eighteenth Church of Christ, Scientist
Seventh Day Adventists
```

2:47 Local branches of fraternal lodges and of unions bear numbers, which should be expressed in arabic numerals following the name:

```
Typographical Union No. 16
American Legion, Department of California, Leon
Robart Post No. 1248
```

2:48   *Street addresses, highways, telephone numbers.* It is preferable to spell out the names of numbered streets under one hundred for the sake of appearance and ease of reading, but street (as well as building) addresses, highway numbers, and telephone numbers should be expressed in figures:

> The address is 10 Eighty–fourth Avenue; the
> telephone number, 321–6530.
>
> 1040 First National Bank Building
>
> California 17   Interstate 80   U.S. Route 30 <u>or</u> U.S. 30

SCIENTIFIC USAGE

2:49   In mathematical, statistical, technical, or scientific text, where physical quantities for distances, lengths, areas, volumes, pressures, and so on, are frequently referred to, all amounts should be expressed in figures, whether they are under or over one hundred:

30 milliliters	2,200 miles
3 cubic feet	125 volts
12 meters	10 picas
60 pounds	10°C, 10.5°C
180 hectares	10° (of arc)

2:50   Note also in technical writing that abbreviations (usually without periods) may be used for distance, length, area, volume, weight, and so on, if the amount is given in numerals:

113 g	50 lb	8.3 ft
32 oz	25 ml	15 kW
137 mm	25–30 min	15 cm^2

THE COMMA WITH NUMBERS

2:51   For the most part, in numbers of one thousand or more, the thousands are marked off with commas:

> 1,500   12,275,500   1,475,525,000

No comma is used, however, in page numbers, street address and telephone numbers, four-digit year numbers, chapter numbers of fraternal organizations and the like, and decimal fractions of less than one.

The Bibliography is on pages 1012-20.

The address is 10314 Hale Avenue; the telephone
number, 238-4728.

In the Coastal district the peel thickness ÷ the
pulp diameter of the Eureka lemon was 0.1911 for
fruit from the top of the tree and 0.2016 for fruit
from the bottom.

The Leon Robart Post was established in 1946.

Note, however, that in year dates of more than four figures,
the comma is employed: 10,000 B.C.

CONTINUED NUMBERS

2:52   The term *continued numbers* (or *inclusive numbers*) refers
to the first and last number of a sequence of numerical
designations, such as pages or years. Continued numbers
are separated by a hyphen in a typewritten work and expressed according to the following scheme, which is based
on the way one normally speaks these numbers:[1]

First Number	Second Number	Examples
Less than 100	Use all digits	3–10; 71–72
100 or multiple	Use all digits	100–104; 600–613
More than 100 but less than 110 (in multiples of 100)	Use changed part only (i.e., omit 0)	107–8; 1002–3
More than 109 (in multiples of 100)	Use last two digits (or all if more than last two digits change)	321–25; 415–532; 1536–38; 1890–1954

The principal use of the foregoing scheme is for page numbers and other numbered parts of written works, and for
inclusive year dates:

pp. 2-14, 45-46, 125-26, 200-210, 308-9

the years 1933-36 of the Great Depression

the Napoleonic victories of 1800-1801

[1]The table is taken from the University of Chicago *Manual of Style*, 12th
ed., p. 205.

PLURALS

2:53   Plurals of numbers expressed in figures are formed by the addition of *s* alone (i.e., not apostrophe and *s*):

K-70s will be on West German roads in the 1970s.

Pilots of the 747s undergo special training.

There was a heavy demand to trade 6½s for the new 8¼s.

2:54   Plurals of spelled-out numbers are formed like the plurals of other nouns:

There were many more twelves and fourteens than thirty-twos, thirty-fours, and thirty-sixes on sale.

Most of the women were in their thirties or forties.

ENUMERATIONS

2:55   *Run on in text.* Numbers (or letters) used to enumerate items in text stand out better when they are set in parentheses, either double or single, than when they are followed by periods:

He gave three reasons for his resignation: (1) age, 63, (2) gradually failing eyesight, and (3) desire to live under less pressure.

2:56   *Beginning a new line or paragraph.* When numbered items in an enumeration without subdivisions begin each on a new line, they are most often indicated by arabic numerals followed by a period. The items may be treated like the paragraphs of the text, that is, given paragraph indention and the runover lines begun at the margin:

> 1. The nature of the relationship between library quality and library use

Or they may be set flush with the margin, and the runover lines aligned with the first line of substantive matter:

> 9. Selective initial dissemination of published material--a direct responsibility of the library
>
> 10. Arrangement and organization of the collection

In both styles, periods following numerals must be aligned. Periods at the ends of lines should be omitted, whether or not the items are composed of complete sentences (see par. 3:55).

2:57   *In outline form.* For an outline or other enumeration in which there are subdivisions, the following scheme of notation and indention is recommended. It is not necessary to use a capital roman numeral for the first level when there are fewer divisions than shown in the example. The first level may well begin with A or with 1 (arabic one):

```
I.  Wars of the Nineteenth Century
    A.  United States
        1.  Civil War, 1861-65
            a)  Causes
                (1)  Slavery
                    (a)  Compromise
                        i)  Missouri Compromise
                       ii)  Compromise of 1850

II. Under the head of . . .
    A.  Under the head of . . .
        1.  Under the head of . . .
                ETC.
```

3 Spelling and Punctuation

SPELLING

3:1 Spelling should accord with the best American usage and must be consistent — except, of course, in quotations, where the original must be followed exactly. The authority recommended for spelling and for syllabication (which generally determines the division of words at the ends of lines) is *Webster's Third New International Dictionary* or its abridgment, *Webster's Seventh New Collegiate Dictionary* (use first spelling where there is a choice). For the spelling of personal names, reference should be made to *Webster's Biographical Dictionary,* and of geographical names, to *Webster's Geographical Dictionary.*

PLURALS

3:2 *Proper names.* Plurals of the names of persons and of other capitalized names are formed by the addition of *s* or *es* without the change of a final *y* to *i* as required for common nouns.

3:3 Add *s* to all names except those ending in *s, x,* or *z,* or in *ch* or *sh*:

```
the Andersons      the Costellos      the Frys
the Bradleys       the Joyces         the Pettees
```

3:4 Add *es* to names ending in *s, x,* or *z,* or in *ch* or *sh*:

```
the Rosses         the Coxes          the Marshes
the Jenkinses      the Rodriguezes    the Finches
```

3:5 *Capital letters.* Form the plurals of most single and multiple capital letters used as nouns by adding *s* alone:

```
The three Rs are taught at the two YMCAs.
```

3:6   *Small letters.* Form the plurals of all small letters, of capital letters with periods, and of capital letters that would be confusing if *s* alone were added, by adding an apostrophe and *s*:

```
All the examples were labeled by letter; the a's
were tested first, the b's second, and so on.
```

```
The B.A.'s and B.S.'s conferred were almost ten
times the number of M.A.'s, M.S.'s, and Ph.D.'s.
```

```
The A's, I's, and S's in the directory were checked
by one group.
```

POSSESSIVES

3:7   Form the possessive case of a proper name in the singular by adding an apostrophe and *s*:

```
Jones's book      Marx's ideology
Stevens's poems   Diaz's revolt
Kinross's farm    Finch's candidacy
```

But see the exceptions noted below (3:8 and 9):

3:8   The possessive case of the names of Jesus and Moses, and of Greek (or hellenized) names of more than one syllable ending in *es,* is formed by adding an apostrophe alone:

```
Jesus' ministry     Aristophanes' plays
Moses' leadership   Xerxes' victories
```

3:9   For some common nouns as well, a regard for euphony sets aside the rule for forming the possessive by adding an apostrophe and *s,* and instead adds only an apostrophe:

```
for conscience' sake     for appearance' sake
for righteousness' sake
```

3:10   Form the possessive case of a plural proper name (the Bradleys, the Costellos, etc.) by adding an apostrophe to the accepted form of the plural of the name. (See pars. 3.3 and 4.)

```
the Bradleys' house    the Rodriguezes' mine
the Costellos' ranch   the Finches' yacht
```

3:11   Note that although the plurals of prepositional-phrase compounds are formed according to the rule governing the first noun of the compound, as, for example:

```
brothers-in-law    commanders-in-chief    men-of-war
```

the possessive case of the same compound words is:

```
my brother-in-law's business
the commander-in-chief's dispatches
the man-of-war's launching
```

COMPOUND WORDS

3:12   The hyphen is used in many compound words; but which should be hyphenated, which left open, and which spelled as one word is a thorny question. The unabridged Webster's dictionary gives the answer for most noun forms and for many adjective forms. Nevertheless, there are still some noun forms and a good many adjective forms that are not included in the dictionary. Principles of hyphenation for some of these are given in the following paragraphs:

3:13   Compounds made up of a word of relationship plus a noun should be spelled as separate words:

```
brother officer        mother church
father figure          parent organization
foster child           sister ship
```

3:14   Compounds made up of two nouns that are different but of equal importance should be hyphenated:

```
author-critic          artist-inventor
composer-director      architect-painter
city-state             scholar-poet
```

3:15   Compounds ending with *-elect* should be hyphenated except when the name of the office is in two or more words:

```
president-elect    but:   county clerk elect
```

3:16   Combinations of words including a prepositional phrase that describe a character should be hyphenated:

```
stay-at-home                    stick-in-the-mud
Alice-sit-by-the-fire           Puss-in-boots
```

3:17 When spelled out, fractional numbers should be hyphenated unless either numerator or denominator already contains a hyphen:

```
two-thirds          but:   six and two-thirds
one-half                   sixty-five hundredths
```

3:18 Many compounds ending with -*book* have been accepted into the general English vocabulary as single words and are to be found in Webster so spelled; others are treated as two words:

```
checkbook           but:   telephone book
textbook                   pattern book
```

3:19 The same applies to compounds ending in -*house*:

```
clubhouse           but:   business house
greenhouse                 rest house
```

3:20 Spell as separate words adjective forms composed of an adverb ending in -*ly* plus an adjective or a participle:

```
highly developed species     barely breathing bird
newly minted coins           easily seen result
```

3:21 Adjective forms composed of unhyphenated proper names should be written as separate words:

```
Old French                   Modern Greek
Latin American               New Testament
```

3:22 Compounds with *better-, best-, ill-, lesser-, little-, well-,* and the like, should be hyphenated when they precede the noun unless there is a modifier:

```
better-paid job           little-expected aid
best-liked teacher        well-intentioned man
ill-advised step     but: a very well intentioned man
lesser-known evil
```

As predicate adjectives they are generally spelled as two words:

```
The step was ill advised. It was clear that the man
was well intentioned.
```

3:23   An adjective form composed of a present participle preceded by its object should be hyphenated:

```
emotion–producing          thought–provoking
dissension–arousing        vote–getting
```

Noun forms similarly constructed are generally treated as two words:

```
decision making            problem solving
coal mining                food gathering
```

3:24   Chemical terms used as adjectives are spelled as two words, unhyphenated:

```
boric acid solution        hydrogen sulfide gas
sodium chloride crystals   tartaric acid powder
```

3:25   All compound adjectives indicating color should be spelled as separate words:

```
gray green                 ruby red
dark blue                  silver gray
reddish purple             coal black
```

3:26   Compounds with *all-* should be hyphenated whether they precede or follow the noun:

```
all–encompassing aim       all–round leader
all–powerful ruler         all–inclusive title
all–out effort             the evil was all–pervasive.
```

3:27   Hyphenate phrases used as adjectives before a noun:

```
six–to–ten–year–old group  matter–of–fact approach
on–the–job training        wage–price controls
catch–as–catch–can         fringe–benefits demands
attitude
```

3:28   Most compounds made up of adjective plus past participles should be hyphenated before a noun and spelled as two words after a noun:

```
rosy–cheeked boy           fine–grained powder
straight–sided dish        open–handed person
```

<u>but</u>:
For a city child he was beautifully rosy cheeked.

3:29   Adjective forms ending with the suffix *-like* should be spelled as one word except when they are formed from proper names, word-combinations, or words ending with *ll* (double ell):

```
barrellike                    mouselike
camplike                      umbrellalike
museumlike                    lacelike
```
but:
```
Tito-like, doll-like, kitchen-cabinet-like
```

3:30 An adjectival compound composed of a cardinal number and the word *-odd* should be hyphenated before or after the noun:

```
forty-odd                     twenty-five-hundred-odd
175-odd                       fifteen-hundred-odd
```

3:31 An adjectival compound composed of a cardinal number and a unit of measurement should be hyphenated when it precedes a noun:

```
twelve-mile limit             eight-space indention
two-inch margin               100-yard dash
```
but: 10 percent increase

3:32 Adjectival compounds with *-fold* are written as one word, unless figures are used:

```
tenfold                       multifold
```
but: 20-fold

3:33 Noun compounds with *quasi* should be spelled as two words:

```
quasi promise                 quasi honor
```

Adjectival compounds with *quasi-* should be hyphenated whether they come before or after the noun:

```
quasi-religious               quasi-political
```

3:34 The trend in the spelling of compound words has for some years been away from the use of hyphens. Nowhere is this more evident that in words with such common prefixes as *pre-, post-; pro-, anti-; over-, under-; intra-, extra-; infra-, ultra-; sub-, super-; re-; un-; non-; semi-; pseudo-; supra-*:

```
prenuptial                    understaffed
postoperative                 intramural
prowar                        extramural
antirevolutionary             infrared
oversupplied                  ultraviolet
```

```
subatomic                    nonfunctional
supersonic                   semiconscious
reactor                      pseudoreligious
unconcerned                  supramundane
```

Adjectives with these prefixes are spelled as one word—unless the second element is capitalized or is a figure:

```
pro-Arab    un-American    pre-1900
```

or it is necessary to distinguish homonyms:

```
re-cover                    re-create
```

or the second element consists of more than one word:

```
non-food-producing people
pre-nuclear-age civilization
```

DIVISION OF WORDS

GENERAL RULES

3:35 In general, divide words at the ends of lines according to their syllabication as shown in the dictionary (*Webster's Third* or *Webster's Seventh Collegiate* as suggested in par. 3:1). If you use a dictionary other than *Webster's,* you may find that the syllables are separated with a dot, except that, following the accented syllable, the accent mark serves the dual purpose of indicating syllabication as well as stress in pronunciation: *syl·lab·i·ca'tion. Webster's* third edition uses a different scheme: instead of placing an accent mark *after* the accented syllable, it places the mark *before* the syllable in the phonetic transcription.

3:36 In general divide according to pronunciation (rather than derivation). This means that when dividing after an accented syllable, the consonant stays with the vowel when the vowel is short:

```
signif-icant    param-eter      hypoth-esis
philos-ophy     democ-racy      prej-udice
```

but goes with the following syllable when it is long:

```
stu-dent        Mongo-lian      divi-sive
```

3:37 Never divide a combination of letters pronounced as one syllable:

36

```
pro-nounced     ex-traor-di-nary     passed
```

3:38   When *-ing* or *-ed* is added to a word whose final syllable contains the liquid *l* (e.g., *cir·cle, han·dle*), the final syllable of the parent word becomes a part of the added syllable:

```
cir-cling     bris-tling     chuck-ling     han-dling
cir-cled      bris-tled      chuck-led      han-dled
```

3:39   In words where an end consonant is doubled before *-ing* and *-ed,* the division comes between the double consonants:

```
set-ting               con-trol-ling
per-mit-ting           per-mit-ted
```

Note that this rule does not apply to words originally ending in a double consonant:

```
add-ing                in-stall-ing
```

EXCEPTIONS AND SPECIAL RULES

3:40   Some divisions, although syllabically correct, should never be made.

3:41   Never make a one-letter division:

```
Wrong:   a-mong  u-nite  e-nough  man-y
```

3:42   Never divide the syllables *-able* and *-ible*:

```
Wrong:   inevita-ble  permissi-ble  allowa-ble
Right:   inevi-table  permis-sible  allow-able
```

3:43   Never divide the following suffixes:

```
-cious  -geous  -cial  -cion  -sion
-ceous  -gious  -sial  -gion  -tion
        -tious  -tial
```

3:44   Avoid two-letter divisions, especially when the division would give a misleading appearance:

```
Not:   wo-man  of-ten  pray-er  mon-ey  loss-es
```

3:45   Avoid division of hyphenated words except at the hyphen:

```
Not:   self-evi-dent  gov-er-nor-elect  well-in-ten-tioned
```

3:46   Avoid division of a proper name unless it is one in which the correct division is obvious:

Right: Wash-ing-ton   Went-worth   Bond-field   John-son

A biographical dictionary should be consulted before risking division of most proper names.

3:47   Never divide initials used in place of given names. It is best to write given names or initials on the same line as the surname, but it is allowable to place all the initials on one line and the surname on the next:

Wrong: T./S. Eliot   J./B. S. or J. B./S. Haldane
Allowable: T. S./ Eliot   J. B. S./Haldane

3:48   Never divide capital letters used as abbreviations for names of countries or states (U.S., N.Y.); or for names of organizations (YMCA, NATO); or for names of publications or radio or television stations (*PMLA*, KKHI, KQED; but two sets of initials separated by a hyphen, e.g., KRON-FM, may be divided after the hyphen). Similarly, never divide the abbreviations for academic degrees (B.A., M.S., LL.D., Ph.D.).

3:49   Never divide a day of the month from the month, and never divide any such combinations as the following:

£6 4s. 6d.   A.D. 1895   6:40 P.M.   245 mi.   10%

3:50   Never end a line with a divisional mark, such as (*a*) or (1), or with a dollar sign, or an opening quotation mark, or an opening parenthesis, or an opening bracket; and never begin a line with an ending quotation mark, or an ending parenthesis, or an ending bracket, or with any mark of punctuation save only a dash (–).

3:51   For rules on the division of words in foreign languages, consult the University of Chicago Press *Manual of Style,* 12th edition.

PUNCTUATION

3:52   Punctuation in some of its specialized uses is treated elsewhere in this *Manual,* in the chapters on abbreviations and numbers, footnotes, bibliographies, quotations, tables, and

illustrations. Here, the general use of of the various marks
of punctuation in the text is dealt with briefly, the primary
aim being to provide answers to questions that frequently
puzzle writers. The rules are based on those set forth in
the University of Chicago Press *Manual of Style.*

PERIOD

3:53 A period, or full stop, is used at the end of a complete
declarative sentence, a moderately imperative sentence,
and a sentence containing an indirect question:

They took the short road into the village.

Take the short road.

The driver asked which road he should take.

3:54 A period denoting an abbreviation and coming at the end
of a sentence may serve also as the closing period. If the
sentence ends with a question mark or an exclamation
point, the abbreviation period is retained:

The meeting adjourned at 5:30 P.M.

Was the committee called for 8:00 P.M.?

How incredible that the speaker should have given
the date as 700 B.C.!

3:55 The period is omitted at the ends of items in a vertical
list or enumeration, whether or not the items are composed
of sentences:

1. The securities markets
2. The securities industry
3. The securities industry in the economy

1. Emphasis is on the discovery of truth
2. Emphasis is on the useful
3. Emphasis is on form and harmony
4. Emphasis is on love of people, especially the
    altruistic and philanthropic aspects of love
5. Emphasis is on power, whether within or without
    the narrow field of politics
6. Emphasis is on unity

3:56 Omit periods at the ends of all the following: (1) display
headings for chapters, tables, plates, and so on; (2) any

subheading that is typed on a line by itself; (3) superscriptions and legends; (4) boxheadings and cut-in headings in tables; (5) address and date lines in communications, and signatures.

3:57   Periods in series (ellipsis points) are used to mark omissions in quoted matter (see pars. 5:16–23), and to guide the eye (period leaders) in relating items in one column of a table to relevant items in opposite columns (see pars. 10:23, 10:26).

QUESTION MARK

3:58   A question mark is used at the end of a whole sentence containing a query or at the end of a query making up part of a sentence:

What has been the result of these studies?

Would the teacher—transplant idea catch on in countries other than Germany? was the question the rejects were asking.

The question put by the Board was, Would the taxpayers vote another bond issue that would raise their taxes?

Note the capitalization of the first word of the sentence that asks the question, even though it is included in another sentence.

3:59   Courtesy disguises as a question such requests as the following, which should end with a period rather than a question mark:

Will you please submit my request to the appropriate office.

3:60   A question mark may be used to indicate uncertainty:

The Italian painter Niccolò dell'Abbate (1512?–1571) assisted in the decorations at Fontainebleau.

EXCLAMATION POINT

3:61   An exclamation point is used to mark an outcry or an emphatic or ironical comment (avoid overuse of this de-

40

vice). Like the question mark, it may occur within a declarative sentence:

```
What havoc was wrought by hurricane Agnes!

"Incredible!" he exclaimed, "I could hardly believe
my senses. Both houses actually passed major bills
on the opening day!"

"It is really too kind of you to warn me of the
slights I am about to encounter!"

"I saw my sixteen-year-old son leap to his feet--
if only I could have stopped him!--and loudly
challenge the speaker."
```

3:62 Do not use an exclamation point to call attention to an error in a quotation, but place the word *sic* enclosed in square brackets after the error (see par. 5:40).

COMMA

3:63 Although the comma indicates the smallest interruption in continuity of thought or sentence structure, when it is correctly used it does more for ease of reading and ready understanding than any other mark of punctuation.

3:64 In sentences containing two independent clauses joined by a coordinating conjunction (*and, but, or, nor, for*), a comma is usually placed before the conjunction. This is not a hard-and-fast rule, however; where the sentence is short and clarity not an issue, no comma is needed.

```
Most young Europeans spend their holidays in other
European countries, and many students take vacation
jobs abroad.

I do not think we can conclude that dissent leads
to counter-revolution, but it seems certain that
dissent, in itself, does not constitute a revolution.

This silence is not surprising, for in those circles
Modernism is still regarded with suspicion.

But:
John arrived early and Mary came an hour later.
```

3:65 Do not use a comma before a conjunction joining the parts of a compound predicate (i.e., two or more verbs having the same subject):

```
The agencies should design their own monitoring
networks and evaluate the data derived from them.
```

They do not self-righteously condemn such societies
but attempt rather to refute them theoretically.

3:66   A series of three or more words, phrases, or clauses (like
this) takes a comma between each of the elements and
before a conjunction separating the last two:

New York, Chicago, and Los Angeles were the cities
mentioned.

She asserted that dishes had been broken, cutlery
lost, and carpets and upholstery damaged beyond
possibility of renovation.

3:67   No commas should be used, however, when the elements
in a series are all joined by conjunctions:

For dessert the menu offered peaches or strawberries
or melon.

3:68   A series of three or more words, phrases, or clauses ending
with the expression *and so forth* or *and so on* or *and the
like* or *etc.* should have commas both preceding and following the expression:

You can improve wages, hours, conditions, benefits,
and so on, as part of the cure.

The basket was overflowing with corn, beans, squash,
carrots, etc., from his own garden.

3:69   When commas occur within one or more of the elements
of a series, semicolons instead of commas should be used
to separate the elements:

Three cities that have had notable success with
the program are Hartford, Connecticut; Kalamazoo,
Michigan; and Pasadena, California.

The percentages of failures were as follows:
Class A, 7 percent; Class B, 13 percent; and
Class C, 20 percent.

3:70   A comma may be used to mark an omission of a word or
words made clear by the context:

In spring and fall there is hiking here; in
summer, sailing; in winter, skiing.

Sometimes, the construction is sufficiently clear without
the commas as well as the semicolons (which the use of

the commas makes necessary), and simpler punctuation is used:

Three students were from India, two from Turkey, and eight from Japan.

3:71   Use commas to set off a nonrestrictive clause or phrase following a main clause. An element is nonrestrictive if it can be omitted without altering the meaning of the main clause:

These books, which are placed on reserve in the library, are required reading for the course.

The clause is nonrestrictive, since the meaning of the main clause, "These books are required reading for the course," is unchanged if the parenthetical clause is omitted. But in the following sentence, the clause identifies the books placed on reserve as those "that are required reading for the course," and the clause is therefore restrictive. No commas should be used:

The books that are required reading for the course are placed on reserve in the library.

3:72   A word, phrase, or clause in apposition to a noun may also be restrictive or nonrestrictive. When it is nonrestrictive, it is set off by commas:

His brother, a Harvard graduate, transferred to Princeton for a program in theology.

A one-time officer in the foreign legion, the man hoped to escape further military duty.

If, however, the appositive limits the meaning of the noun and is therefore restrictive, no commas should be used:

The Danish philosopher Kierkegaard asks, "What is anxiety?"

The motion picture Becket is adapted from the play by Jean Anouilh.

3:73   Similarly, commas are generally used to set off a phrase indicating place of residence, immediately following a personal name:

Representative Sidney R. Yates, of Illinois, was the first speaker.

Note, however, that the commas should be omitted in those cases where the place name has practically become a part of the person's name:

```
St. Francis of Assisi    John of Austria
```

3:74   The name of a title or position following a person's name should be set off with commas:

```
Norman Cousins, former editor of the Saturday Review,
wrote the editorial "Lunar Meditations."
```

3:75   Set off with commas the individual elements in addresses and names of places:

```
The address is 340 Forest Avenue, Palo Alto,
California 94023.
```

```
The next leg of our trip was to take us to Beirut,
Lebanon, and promised to be the most rewarding.
```

3:76   Set off with commas interjections, transitional adverbs, and the like, when they cause a distinct break in the flow of thought:

```
His statement, therefore, cannot be verified.
That, after all, is a matter of great importance.
Indeed, this is precisely what Martens feared.
It is, perhaps, the best that could be expected.
```

But note that when such elements do not cause a break in continuity and do not require a pause in reading, the commas should be omitted:

```
It is therefore clear that no deposits were made.
This is indeed the crux of the matter.
Perhaps it requires further explication.
```

3:77   In using commas to set off a parenthetical element in the middle of a sentence, the writer must remember to include both commas:

```
Wrong:  The bill, you will be pleased to hear passed
        at the last session.
Right:  The bill, you will be pleased to hear, passed
        at the last session.
Wrong:  The problem of communication is less serious
        it is held, with the new generation than with
        the old.
```

> Right: The problem of communication is less serious,
>   it is held, with the new generation than with
>   the old.

3:78 Use a comma following *namely, that is, for example, i.e.,
e.g.* There must be a punctuation mark before each of these
expressions, but the kind of mark varies with the nature
and complexity of the sentence:

> Two other countries with a combined population of
> 45 million, namely, Greece and Turkey, already are
> half-members.
>
> Christianity really does two things about conditions
> here and now in this world: it tries to make them as
> good as possible—that is, to reform them—but also
> it fortifies you against them insofar as they remain
> bad.
>
> Many people feel resentful because they think they
> have suffered an unjust fate; that is, they look
> upon illness, bereavement, deranged domestic or
> working conditions as being undeserved.
>
> Restrictions on the sulfur content of fuel oil are
> already in effect in some cities (e.g., Paris,
> Milan, Rome, and Stockholm), and the prospect is
> that limits will be imposed sooner or later in
> most cities.

3:79 When a dependent clause or a long participial or prepositional phrase begins a sentence, it is usually followed by
a comma:

> If the insurrection is to succeed, the army and
> the police must stand side by side.
>
> Although there are splendid innovations, life in
> the residential clusters strung out along a city's
> fingers will not be to everyone's taste.
>
> After spending a week in conferences, the commission
> was able to write a report.
>
> Because of traffic delays, the party missed the plane.
>
> Pampering their cars, Europeans spend in the
> neighborhood of 10 percent of their income to
> operate and maintain them.
>
> Faced with the threat of a tight supply situation,
> European governments are casting about for solutions
> to the problem.

3:80   No comma should follow a participial phrase that is part
of the main verb or an adverbial phrase that immediately
precedes the verb it modifies. And a comma is usually
unnecessary after a short prepositional phrase:

```
Strolling through the Temple of Athena were tourists
mostly from Sweden and Denmark.
From the Olympic Tower comes greatly improved TV
reception.
Beneath the Karlsplatz will be a four-level city
within a city.
On Fridays we usually go to our summer place.
For recreation the mayor fishes or sails.
```

3:81   When each of several adjectives preceding a noun modifies
the noun individually, they should be separated with
commas:

```
It was a large, well-placed, beautiful house.
We stroll out into the warm, luminous night.
```

However, if the last adjective *identifies* the noun rather
than merely modifying it, no comma should precede it:

```
Then in the procession came the tall, dignified
third-year students.
His is the large brick house on the corner.
```

3:82   Set off with commas contrasted elements and two or more
complementary or antithetical phrases or clauses referring
to a single word following:

```
The idea, not its expression, is significant.
The harder we run, the more we stay in the same place.
She both delighted in, and was disturbed by, her
new leisure and freedom.
It is a logical, if a harsh, solution to the problem.
```

3:83   Use a comma to separate two identical or closely similar
words:

```
They marched in, in twos.
Whatever is, had best be accepted.
```

3:84   A comma should be used to prevent misreading of such
sentences as the following:

> From the British, educated Indians learned the
> principles of parliamentary democracy.
>
> After eating, the lions yawned and then dozed.

SEMICOLON

3:85 A semicolon marks a greater break in the continuity of a sentence than that indicated by a comma. Use a semicolon between the parts of a compound sentence (two or more independent clauses) when they are not connected by a conjunction:

> More than one hundred planned communities are in
> various stages of completion; many more are on the
> drawing boards.

3:86 If the clauses of a compound sentence are very long and there are commas within them, they should be separated with semicolons even though they are connected by a conjunction:

> Although productivity per man in U.S. industry is
> almost twice that in West European industry, Western
> Europe has an increasingly well-educated young
> labor force; and the crucial point is that knowledge,
> which is transferable between peoples, has become
> by far the most important world economic resource.

3:87 When used transitionally between the clauses of compound sentences, the words *hence, however, indeed, so, then, thus,* and *yet* are considered adverbs, not conjunctions, and should therefore be preceded by semicolons rather than commas:

> There are those who consider freedom basically in
> terms of social and economic egalitarianism; thus,
> reformist governments of the left are inherently
> viewed with greater favor than the status-quo
> regimes of the right.
>
> The idea of a "cultural army" goes far back in Mao's
> works; however, he is not innovating: culture is
> always the reflection of political and social reality.

3:88 For the use of a semicolon instead of a comma, see paragraphs 3:69–70, 3:78.

47

COLON

3:89   The use of the colon in a sentence indicates a discontinuity of grammatical construction greater than that indicated by the semicolon. Whereas the semicolon is used to separate parts that are usually of equal significance, the colon is used to introduce a clause or phrase that expands, clarifies, or exemplifies the meaning of what precedes it:

```
The New World and the Old share the same monumental
urban problems: their populations mount, and in all
industrial nations the migration from country to city
has become a flood.
```

```
People at present seek three main things through
and partly from their governmental systems: peace,
prosperity, and a more cohesively gracious form of
living together.
```

3:90   A colon should be placed at the end of a grammatical element introducing a formal statement, whether the statement is quoted or not. It is usually placed after *following* or *as follows* or *in sum* when the enumerated items or illustrations come immediately after:

```
His "laws" are as follows:
1.  Books are for use
2.  For every reader his book
3.  For every book its reader
```

3:91   As noted elsewhere in this *Manual,* a colon is used between chapter and verse in scriptural references (par. 2:11), between hours and minutes in notations of time (par. 2:42), between place and publisher in footnote and bibliographical references (par. 6:54), and between volume and page reference in citations (par. 6:74).

DASH

3:92   The dash, which in printing is a continuous line, in typescript consists of two hyphens without space between or on either side of them.

3:93   A dash or a pair of dashes may indicate a sudden break in thought that disrupts the sentence structure:

```
The characters in Tom Jones tend to be "flat"--
to use the term E. M. Forster made fashionable--
because there is often little or no sign of conflict.
```

> To this the young man answered--he must have been
> very young--"I will do as you say."

> The American educational adviser often knew about
> the country only that it needed many things,
> including--and this was heady wine--advice from
> him.

3:94 Breaks in faltering speech or interruptions should be indicated by dashes:

> "Well, it's as I said, difficult to explain--but
> the service, being considered so important by us
> Russians--if you were absent--I don't know how to
> put it, people might think--might think--"

> Becky and Ann--where have they gone?

3:95 Use a dash to introduce an element that emphasizes or explains the main clause through repetition of a key word or key words:

> He asked where wisdom was to be found--"the wisdom
> that is above rubies."

> One is expected to cram all this stuff into one's
> mind--cram it all in, whether it's likely to be
> useful or not.

3:96 In a sentence that includes several elements referring to a word that is the subject of a final, summarizing clause, a dash should precede the final clause:

> The statue of the man throwing the discus, the
> charioteer at Delphi, the poetry of Pindar--all
> show the culmination of the great ideal.

> Vietnam, the welfare tangle, inflation--these are
> problems most troubling to concerned citizens.

3:97 A word or phrase set on a line by itself, the meaning of which is completed by two or more parallel elements that follow, may end with a dash:

> On two major propositions the consensus was--
> 1. that the historical function of the library
>   has been as an agency of culture;
> 2. that the selective initial dissemination of
>   published material is a direct responsibility
>   of libraries.

When such parallel elements are run into the text, no dash is used:

> On two major propositions the consensus was (1) that
> the historical function of the library has been as
> an agency of culture and (2) that the selective
> initial dissemination of published material is a
> direct responsibility of libraries.

For the use of numbers to enumerate items in text, see paragraph 2:55.

PARENTHESES

3:98   The principal uses of parentheses in the text of a paper are (1) to set off parenthetical elements, (2) to enclose the source of a quotation or other matter when a footnote is not used for the purpose, and (3) to set off the numbers or letters in an enumeration (like that in this sentence). The first use is a matter of choice, since both commas and dashes are also used to set off parenthetical material. In general, commas are used for material most closely related to the main clause, dashes and parentheses for material more remotely connected. The following examples illustrate some instances where parentheses might be used:

> The conference has (with some malice aforethought)
> been divided into four major areas.

> It is significant that in the Book of Revelation
> (a book Whitehead did not like because of its bloody
> and apocalyptic imagery), the vision of a new heavenly
> city at the end of time has the divine light shine
> so that the nations walk by it, and the "kings of
> the earth shall bring their glory into it" (Rev.
> 21:22–26).

> Each painting depicted some glorious, or vainglorious,
> public occasion of the last hundred years; in each––a
> formal diplomatic banquet, a victory parade, the
> opening of the Burbank Airport in 1931 (clouded by
> a phalanx of tiny Ford Trimotors)––the crowds of
> people were replaced by swarms of ants.

BRACKETS

3:99   Brackets, often called *square brackets,* are used (1) to enclose any interpolation in a quotation (see pars. 5:39–41) and (2) to enclose parenthetical matter within a parenthesis:

```
The book is available in translation (see J. R.
Evans-Wentz, The Tibetan Book of the Dead [Oxford:
Oxford University Press, 1927]).
```

3:100 If within the bracket further parenthesis is required, use parentheses again:

```
The various arguments advanced (these include certain
anonymous writers [Public Economy (New York, 1848)])
may be formulated thus: . . .
```

OTHER PUNCTUATION MARKS

3:101 The use of quotation marks is described in paragraphs 5:9–14.

3:102 The hyphen, sometimes considered a mark of punctuation, is discussed in paragraphs 3:12–51 (compound words and word division) and paragraph 2:52 (continued numbers).

MULTIPLE PUNCTUATION

3:103 The term *multiple punctuation* means the conjunction of two marks of punctuation—for example, a period and a closing parenthesis. Where such conjunction occurs, certain rules must be observed concerning (1) whether to omit one mark or the other (as a period when an abbreviation ends a sentence, see par. 3:54) or (2) which mark to put first when both marks are kept.

3:104 A comma is generally omitted following a stronger mark of punctuation:

```
If he had watched "What's My Line?" he would have
known the answer.
The owner yelled, "Get out!" and the robber fled.
```

3:105 The comma is retained after the dash in certain special instances, and always when it falls after an abbreviation with a period:

```
"If you were absent--I don't know how to put it--
people might think--might think--," Vasily finished
on a rising note of inquiry.
Never use the abbreviations St., Ave., or Rte. in
formal correspondence.
```

51

3:106   Two marks of punctuation fall in the same place chiefly where quotation marks, parentheses, or brackets are involved.

3:107   In American usage, with quotation marks, a final comma or period always goes *inside* (i.e., before the closing quotation mark), whether it is part of the quoted matter or not. Question marks and exclamation points go inside if they are part of the quoted matter, outside if they pertain to the entire sentence of which the quotation is a part. Semicolons and colons go outside the quotation marks, as part of the sentence containing the quotation. (If the quoted passage ends with a semicolon or a colon in the original, the mark would normally be changed to a period or a comma to accord with the structure of the main sentence.)

Every public official and every professional person
is called upon "to join in the effort to bring
justice and hope to all our people."

The probable is not what accords with some hypothesis
about the "existing laws of human affairs," nor is
it what accords with the "ordinary processes of life."

Even this small advance begins to raise the question,
"What in effect is our true image, our real likeness?"

Thus a novel is not analyzed, . . . until we have
discovered its place in the mind of the novelist
(is this the "intentional fallacy"?), in the movement
of the age.

Do we accept Jefferson's concept of "a natural
aristocracy among men"?

Charged by a neighbor with criminal mistreatment
of her child and threatened with police action,
the woman retorted, "Just let you call the police,
and you'll regret it to your dying day!"

How dreadful it was to hear her reply--calmly--"We'll
let the law decide that"!

He made the point that "in every human attitude and
choice we make, we are taking an attitude toward
Everyman"; and then enlarged upon the point in a
particularly telling way.

Rome's one planned subcenter, EUR, is "almost a
self-contained city": it governs itself and provides
its own services.

3:108   In fields where it is the practice to use single quotation marks to set off special terms, a period or comma follows the closing quotation mark:

> Some contemporary theologians were proclaiming the 'death of God'.

But in the following title of an article which includes the title of another article, the period is correctly placed within the closing quotation marks, both single and double:

> The article to which he referred is in the Journal of Political Economy: "Comment on 'How to Make a Burden of the Public Debt.'"

3:109   When a complete sentence enclosed in parentheses or brackets stands alone, the terminal period for that sentence is placed within the parentheses or brackets. When the parenthetical sentence appears inside another sentence, however, the period is omitted:

> We have already noted similar motifs in Japan. (Significantly, very similar motifs can also be found in the myths and folk tales of Korea.)

> The car crept up the driveway (I saw it turn in from the road) and paused just short of the entrance.

3:110   No punctuation should be placed between a parenthetical element and the element it modifies or to which it is closely connected. Therefore, internal sentence punctuation normally follows the parenthetical element and no punctuation precedes it:

> Myths have been accepted as literally true, then as allegorically true (by the Stoics), as confused history (by Euhemerus), as priestly lies (by the philosophers of the Enlightenment), as imitative agricultural ritual mistaken for propositions (in the days of Frazer).

> "If he [the believer] stops here [with the base statement of election with reference only to himself], who shall blame him?"

> Stephen Enke, Economics for Development (Englewood Cliffs, N.J.: Prentice-Hall, 1963), p. 91.

> Madrid received via Brussels not only its correspondence from England (the most important

focus of Spanish diplomacy in the period),
northern Europe, and the emperor, but often even
the dispatches from Rome.

It is clear that one of the main motives was to
reduce the speaking roles (even as a new role, that
of the Clown, was being built up); and the action
has been padded in several places.

Deep underground here, a "forum" will be built
(like the galleries of Naples and Milan): elegant
stores, cinemas, and restaurants as fine as any of
their Italian counterparts.

3:111 Numbers or letters in an enumeration in the text belong
with the items following them, and therefore sentence
punctuation precedes them and no punctuation mark comes
between them and the item to which they apply:

He gave three reasons for resigning: (1) advanced
age, (2) failing health, and (3) a desire to travel.

3:112 Square brackets used to set off words or phrases supplied
to fill in incomplete parts of a quotation (par. 5:39) or dates
supplied in citations (par. 6:67) are ignored in punctuating
— i.e., punctuate as if there were no brackets:

The states have continued to respond to "the federal
stimulus for improvement in the scope and amount of
categorical assistance programs. . . . [Yet] Congress
has adhered to its original decision that residence
requirements were necessary."

New York: Macmillan Co., [1910].

4 Capitalization, Underlining, and Other Matters of Style

CAPITALIZATION

4:1 In all languages written in the Latin alphabet proper nouns —the names of persons and places—are capitalized:

```
John and Jane Doe     Niagara Falls
```

4:2 In English, proper adjectives—adjectives derived from proper nouns—are also capitalized:

```
European     Machiavellian
```

4:3 But proper nouns and adjectives that have lost their original meanings and become part of everyday language are not capitalized:

```
french doors     india ink
```

OTHER NAMES

4:4 Except for proper names the practice of capitalization varies widely. Names of organizations and political divisions are usually capitalized, but not always. Titles of persons are sometimes capitalized but by no means always. In American usage the tendency is wherever possible *not* to capitalize. The writer of a paper should decide, before the final typescript is prepared, which terms are to be capitalized and which are not. Inconsistency in the matter is a sign of sloppy writing. Detailed suggestions for capitalization of many terms occurring in run of text may be found in chapter 7 of the University of Chicago Press *Manual of Style*. The following paragraphs discuss the

55

capitalization of titles of written works, the problem encountered most frequently by writers of papers.

TITLES OF WORKS

4:5   In giving titles of published works in text, footnotes, or bibliography, the spelling of the original should be retained, but capitalization and punctuation may be altered to conform to the style used in the paper. In most scientific fields capitalization is kept to a minimum (see chap. 12 for examples). In the humanities and most of the social sciences, however, it is customary to capitalize titles according to the rules given in the following paragraphs.

4:6   In the titles of English works, capitalize the first and last words and all words except articles, prepositions, and coordinate conjunctions:

Economic Effects of the War upon Women and Children

"What It Is All About"

How to Overcome Urban Blight: A Twentieth-Century Problem

Note that the subtitle, following a colon, is capitalized the same way as the main title.

4:7   Rules for capitalizing compound words vary widely. In general, capitalize both elements of a compound word that is hyphenated for syntactical reasons, such as *Twentieth-Century* when used as an adjective as in the last example in par. 4:6; capitalize only the first element of a compound word that is a separate word in its own right, such as *Self-sustaining, Mother-in-law.*

4:8   The original capitalization of long titles of works published in earlier centuries is usually retained:

The precedents of general issues, and the most usual special pleas; precedents of replications, rejoinders, demurrers, &c; a synopsis of practice, or general view of the time when the proceedings in an action should be carried on in the Court of King's Bench and Common Pleas.

4:9   In the titles of French, Italian, and Spanish works, capitalize the first word and proper nouns:

Dictionnaire illustré de la mythologie et des
antiquités grecques et romaines

Bibliografia di Roma nel' Cinquecento

Historia de la Orden de San Gerónimo

Since some romance language departments may have different rules on capitalizing titles, it is well to check the matter before typing a paper in these fields.

4:10   In German titles, capitalize the first word and all nouns, both common and proper, but not proper adjectives:

Reallexikon zur deutschen Kunstgeschichte

4:11   In Greek and Latin titles, capitalize the first word and proper nouns and proper adjectives:

Iphigeneia hē en Taurois

Speculum Romanae magnificentiae

4:12   An exception is made for modern works with Latin titles, which usually are capitalized as though they were English:

Acta Apostolicae Sedis   Quo Vadis?

4:13   Such parts of a work as *contents, preface, foreword, introduction, bibliography, appendix* should not be capitalized in passing references:

A foreword may be included if desired.
The paper should include a bibliography.

But when references are made to a *specific work,* the name of the part is capitalized or not, in accordance with the rule in paragraphs 4:14 and 4:15 below.

4:14   When the reference is made to a part of which there is but one in the work (e.g., Preface, Table of Contents, Bibliography), the name of that part is capitalized:

The Preface to this popular work was written by
Lionel Trilling.

> The Table of Contents lists only chapter numbers and titles.
>
> The Bibliography is classified into works by the author and works about the author.

4:15   But when the reference is to a part of which there is more than one, such as chapters, parts, figures, tables, the name of the part is not capitalized:

> "Thinking French" is the title of chapter 6.
>
> The physical conditions of the experiment are listed in table 2.
>
> Copies of supporting documents are in appendix 3.

If there was but *one* appendix, the word would be capitalized:

> The Appendix contains the supporting documents.

UNDERLINING AND QUOTATION MARKS FOR TITLES

4:16   In all fields except some of the sciences, some titles of written works, published or unpublished, and some other kinds of names and titles are underlined (to indicate a title that would be italicized in printing); others are enclosed in double quotation marks, and still others are capitalized but neither underlined nor enclosed in quotation marks. The general rule is to underline the titles of *whole* published works and to put the titles of *parts* of these works in quotation marks. Titles of unpublished material are also in quotation marks. Titles of series and manuscript collections, and various kinds of descriptive titles, are neither underlined nor in quotation marks.

BOOKS AND PERIODICALS

4:17   Underline the titles of books, pamphlets, bulletins, periodicals (magazines, journals, newspapers). It should be noted that although a published work is usually thought of as set in type and printed in conventional form, it may be a typewritten script reproduced by mimeograph, multigraph, or one of the lithographic processes, or it may be published in microform (see par. 6:118). *If the work bears a* *publisher's imprint*, it should be treated as published rather than unpublished material; that is, the title should be underlined wherever it is referred to.

4:18   Titles of chapters or other titled divisions of a book, short stories and essays, and articles in periodicals are set in quotation marks.

The First Circle, chap. 27, "A Puzzled Robot"

"The New Feminism," Saturday Review

"Amazing Amazon Region," New York Times

"The Demon Lover," Fifty Years: A Retrospective Collection . . .

Part 4 of the Systematic Theology, "Life and the Spirit"

BOOK SERIES AND EDITIONS

4:19   Titles of series and names of editions are neither underlined nor put in quotation marks:

Michigan Business Studies

Modern Library edition

DISSERTATIONS AND PAPERS

4:20   Titles of unpublished theses and dissertations and other papers are set in quotation marks:

"Intergenerational Family Helping Patterns"
(Ph.D. dissertation, University of Minnesota, 1964)

"Costing of Human Resource Development," paper presented at the Conference of the International Economics Association

"One Man's CBI: A Different Kind of War," unpublished MSS, Hoover Library, Stanford, Calif.

MANUSCRIPT COLLECTIONS

4:21   Names of manuscript collections and archives and designations such as *diary, memorandum*, etc., are not underlined or set in quotation marks:

```
British Museum, Harleian MSS
Hoover Library, Stanford, California, unpublished MSS
```

See also pars. 6:119–20.

SACRED SCRIPTURE

4:22   The titles of books of sacred scripture — Bible, Koran, Talmud, Upanishads, Vedas, etc. — and the names of books of the Bible and of the Apocrypha are neither underlined nor set in quotation marks:

```
the King James Version of the Bible
The Book of Daniel is a part of the apocalyptic
literature of the Bible.
```

POEMS

4:23   Titles of long poems are underlined; titles of short poems are in quotation marks:

```
Milton's Paradise Lost
```

```
"Pied Beauty," in The Oxford Book of Modern Verse
```

PLAYS AND MOTION PICTURES

4:24   Titles of plays and motion pictures are underlined:

```
O'Neill's The Iceman Cometh
the movie Citizen Kane
```

RADIO AND TELEVISION PROGRAMS

4:25   Titles of radio and television programs are set in quotation marks:

```
CBS's "My Three Sons"
"Echoes and Encores" on KKHI
```

MUSICAL COMPOSITIONS

4:26   Actual titles of long musical compositions — operas, oratorios, symphonies, ballets, tone poems — are underlined;

60

titles of short compositions—songs, piano pieces, and the
like—are set in quotation marks:

Mozart's The Magic Flute

Handel's Messiah [not The Messiah]

Beethoven's Eroica symphony; or Symphony no. 5
(Eroica)

Stravinsky's ballet The Rite of Spring

Sibelius's tone poem Finlandia

the song "My Robin Is to the Greenwood Gone"

"Belle Nuit," from Les contes d'Hoffmann

4:27   Many musical compositions have no title as such but are
identified by the name of the musical form and the key
and sometimes the number. Such designations are neither
underlined nor in quotation marks. When an attributed
title is given as well, it is put in quotation marks and parentheses after the designation of form and key:

Beethoven's Sonata in D Major, op. 128

Bach's Prelude and Fugue in E-flat ("St. Anne")

ART WORKS

4:28   Actual titles of paintings, drawings, and sculpture are
underlined. Purely descriptive, or attributed, titles are
not.

Rembrandt's etching Abraham's Sacrifice

van Gogh's painting The Harvest

Bernini's sculpture Apollo and Daphne

But:
Mona Lisa

Victory of Samothrace

SHIPS AND AIRCRAFT

4:29   Actual names of ships, aircraft, and spacecraft are underlined. Designations of make, etc., are not:

S.S. Constitution	Spirit of St. Louis
H.M.S. Saranac	Apollo XIII

61

FOREIGN WORDS AND PHRASES

4:30   Underline foreign words and phrases that are used in English text without quotation marks:

> Clearly, this . . . leads to the idea of Übermensch and also to the theory of the acte gratuit and surrealism.

See also par. 4:34.

4:31   A quotation entirely in a foreign language is not underlined. In the following sentence, the words *le pragmatisme* are underlined within the English text, but the words of the quotation, all in French, are properly not underlined:

> The confusion of le pragmatisme is traced to the supposed failure to distinguish "les propriétés de la valeur en général" from the incidental.

4:32   In the following quotation, the writer has underlined some words used as examples. The person using the quotation in English text must observe the author's usage, since a quotation must always be reproduced exactly as it appears in the original:

> Reviewing Mr. Wright's book, Professor Nichols writes: "Quand j'ai dû analyser le style de Wright . . . j'ai été frappé par l'emploi ironique de ses conjonctions causales (à cause, parce que, etc.)."

4:33   Foreign titles preceding proper names, and foreign names of persons, places, institutions, and the like, are not underlined:

Père Grou	the Puerto del Sol
M. Jacquet, Ministre de Travaux	the Vienna Staatsoper
	the Quai d'Orsay
the Académie Française	the Gare du Nord
the Teatro real	the Casa de los Guzmanes

4:34   Do not underline in English text those foreign words which by continued use in English have become anglicized. Listed below are some of the more common anglicized words. Note that some words in the list do not show the accent marks proper to their native forms. In others the accent marks are retained and must be inserted in ink, by hand, unless your typewriter has them. It is never permissible to use an apostrophe for a grave or an acute accent mark; it is permissible, however, to use a comma for a cedilla and quotation marks for an umlaut.

a posteriori	kapellmeister
a priori	laissez faire
ad hoc	mea culpa
ad infinitum	mélange
ante bellum	ménage
apropos	milieu
attaché	mores
barranca	naïveté
beau ideal	par excellence
bête noire	pasha
blitzkrieg	per annum
bona fide	per capita
bourgeoisie	percent
carte blanche	per se
chargé d'affaires	pro rata
cliché	rapport
communiqué	rapprochement
contretemps	recherché
coup d'état	regime
coup de grâce	remuda
debris	résumé
denouement	role
de rigueur	status quo
dilettante	subpoena
élan	tête-à-tête
émigré	Übermensch
entree	versus
entrepreneur	via
ex officio	vice versa
exposé	vis-à-vis
façade	visa
genre	Weltanschauung
habeas corpus	weltschmerz

4:35   In general, foreign words and expressions not included in the foregoing list should be underlined. (The latest editions of Webster's dictionaries do not indicate whether a foreign word has been accepted into the English vocabulary.)

5   Quotations

5:1   In general, direct quotations should correspond exactly with the originals in wording, spelling, capitalization, and punctuation. Exceptions to the general rule are discussed under "Ellipses" (pars. 5:16–38), "Interpolations" (pars. 5:39–41), and "Italics" (par. 5:42).

PROSE

5:2   Short, direct prose quotations should be incorporated into the text of the paper and enclosed in double quotation marks. But in general a prose quotation of two or more sentences which at the same time runs to four or more typewritten lines should be set off from the text in single spacing and indented in its entirety four spaces from the left marginal line, with no quotation marks at beginning or end. A quotation so treated is called a *block quotation* in this *Manual*. Exceptions to this rule are allowable when, for purposes of emphasis or of comparison, it is desirable to block quotations of less than four typewritten lines in length. Paragraph indention in the original text should be indicated by a four-space indention. (See sample pages, par. 13:42.) Double-space between the text and the block quotation, but single-space between the paragraphs of the quotation, except when quoting passages from different works of the same author, or from different authors, in which cases double-space between the separate passages.

POETRY

5:3   Quotations of poetry two or more lines in length should normally be set off from the text, line for line as in the original, single-spaced, and centered on the page:

> The river sweats
> Oil and tar
> The barges drift
> With the turning tide
> Red sails
> Wide
> To leeward, swing on the heavy spar.
>   T. S. Eliot, "The Waste Land"

5:4   If the lines of the poem are too long to be centered on the page, all the lines should be indented four spaces, with any runover lines indented another four spaces:

> The yellow bird sings in their tree and
>   makes my heart dance with gladness.
> We both live in the same village, and
>   that is our one piece of joy.
>   Rabindranath Tagore,
>   "The Yellow Bird Sings"

5:5   In quoting excerpts of poems, as shown above, use no quotation marks at beginning and end. Use quotation marks, however, when giving successive quotations from poems by the same author or by different authors; place quotation marks at the beginning of every stanza and at the end of only the last. Leave an extra space between stanzas of a poem, between excerpts from different poems of the same author, and between excerpts from different authors.

5:6   It is sometimes desirable to insert a line or two of verse directly into text. For example, a writer who is making a critical examination of a poem may find this method of quoting well suited to his purpose. Quotation marks are placed at the beginning and the end of the line or lines quoted, and, if there is more than one line, a virgule (/) is used to separate them:

> In the valley the mariners find life's purposes
> reduced to the simple naturalistic proposition,
> "All things have rest, and ripen toward the
> grave; / In silence, ripen, fall, and cease."

EPIGRAPHS

5:7   When used at the heads of chapters, epigraphs are given the same indention as the paragraphs of the paper, and they are not enclosed in quotation marks. The source is given below the epigraph and is aligned to end with it at the right margin.

> A storm of mosquitoes may create a noise like thunder.
>
> Old Chinese saying

QUOTATIONS IN FOOTNOTES

5:8   Whether run in the body of the footnote or indented and set off from it, all quoted matter appearing in footnotes is enclosed in quotation marks:

> [1]"He leaves a terrible blank behind him and I have a horrid lonely feeling knowing that he is gone" (Field-Marshal Lord Alanbrooke, Diary, 18 April 1940 [MS, Personal Files]). Writing of Dill somewhat later, Brooke expressed a strong feeling of admiration and affection:
>
>> "I know of no other soldier in the whole of my career who inspired me with greater admiration and respect. An exceptionally clear, well-balanced brain, an infinite capacity for work, unbounded charm of personality, but, above all, an unflinching straightness of character. . . . I owe him an infinite debt for all I learned from him" (idem, "Notes on My Life" [MS, Personal Files], vol. II, p. 66).

QUOTATION MARKS

5:9   Direct quotations other than block quotations as described in paragraphs 5:2–4 require double quotation marks at beginning and end. If the quoted passage itself contains a quotation that is set off with double quotation marks, those marks must be changed to single (see par. 5:14). In a block quotation, however, where no marks are used at beginning and end, the double quotation marks that appear within the original matter are retained.

5:10   In addition to their use with quotations from other sources, double quotation marks are used to set off titles (see pars. 4:16–27) and single words, letters, or numbers in certain contexts:

Twenty—one papers were prepared under the topics
"Background," "Relation to Card Catalogs," "Tech-
niques," "Standards," "Applications."

The enumerations may be either numbered "1," "2,"
"3," etc., or lettered "a," "b," "c," etc.

In some fields—linguistics, theology—it is accepted practice to use single quotation marks to set off words and
concepts being discussed:

<u>kami</u> 'hair, beard'

The variables of quantification, 'something',
'nothing', . . .

See also par. 3:108.

5:11   In quoting a letter (correspondence), quotation marks are
placed at the beginning of each element of the address, of
the salutation, of each paragraph, of the complimentary
close, and of the signature. Closing quotation marks appear
only after the signature:[1]

> "Baltimore, Maryland
> "June 1, 1965

"The University of Chicago
"Chicago, Illinois

"Gentlemen:

"Will you kindly refer my request for information
concerning the next series of public lectures on
Far Eastern art to the proper office.

> "Very truly yours,
> "Clyde L. Brown"

5:12   Similarly, in quoting an outline or an enumeration, quotation marks are placed before each unit and at the end of
only the last:

Their outline for the third—year course is as follows:
"III. Predicate—element concept

---

[1]The use of quotation marks as directed here and in paragraphs 5:12 and
5:13 does not reverse the rule given in paragraph 5:2, which calls for the
indention and single-spacing of long quotations and the omission of
quotation marks at beginning and end. But when a paper includes the
writer's own outlines or similar material—single-spaced and indented—as
well as the same kind of materials quoted from other writers, it is advisable
to enclose all quoted matter in quotation marks.

```
"A.  Verb
     "1.  Forms and uses of verb 'to be'
     "2.  Tense
          "a)  Present perfect
          "b)  Past perfect"
```

And for an enumeration in which the items are treated as paragraphs, note the following:

```
"1.  Book selection
"2.  Arrangement and organization of the collection
"3.  Guidance to readers"
```

5:13   For a quotation that includes headings and subheadings, quotation marks are placed before each heading and subheading as well as before each paragraph, with the closing quotation marks coming only at the end of the part quoted:

"CHAPTER II

"THE DEVELOPMENT OF A RACE RELATIONS

ACTION—STRUCTURE

"Race Relations in the British
Isles: 1700 to the First World War

```
    "From the defeat of the Spanish Armada in 1588
until the abolition of slavery throughout the British
Empire in 1833, the economy of Britain was tied,
in some measure, to the fortunes of the African slave
trade. . . .
    "There were individuals among both the adherents
of Conservative and Liberal—humanitarian ideological
systems who felt that, . . ."
```

5:14   For a quotation within a quotation, single quotation marks are used; for another quotation within that one, double marks are again used; if yet another, single marks, and so on:

```
The chairman reported as follows: "The mayor's
representative has replied: 'I am authorized by
the Chamber of Commerce to make this offer, their
provision stating, "The jobs shall be made available
provided that the committee guarantee all the means
for receiving applications." That guarantee has been
made and a procedure outlined for taking job
applications.' Our thanks go to the mayor for his
handling of our committee's request."
```

PUNCTUATION WITH QUOTATION MARKS

5:15   Periods and commas should be placed inside quotation marks (even when the quotation marks enclose only one letter or figure); semicolons and colons, outside. Question marks and exclamation marks should be placed outside the quotation marks unless the question or the exclamation occurs within the quotation itself. In the first example below, the question is not posed within the quotation, but in the sentence as a whole, and the question mark properly belongs after the closing quotation mark. In the other two examples, the question mark in one and the exclamation mark in the other clearly belong within the quotations:

```
Does he precisely show "evil leading somehow to good"?
One may well ask: "Is it really necessary to lose
the world in order to find ourselves?"
The cries of "Long live the king!" echoed down the
broad avenues.
```

See also pars. 3:107–8, 5:28–29.

ELLIPSES

5:16   Any omission of words, phrases, or paragraphs in quoted matter is indicated by ellipsis points, which are period dots, not asterisks (stars). There should be a space before each dot, unless the first dot is a period, and a space also after the last if a word follows. Since ellipsis points stand for words omitted from the quotation itself, they are always placed *within* the quotation marks.

OMISSION WITHIN A SENTENCE

5:17   An omission within a sentence is shown by three spaced dots:

```
In conclusion he stated: "What we require to be
taught . . . is to be our own teachers."
```

5:18   If other punctuation comes immediately before the ellipsis, it is placed next to the word:

```
"We are fighting for the holy cause of Slavdom, . . .
for freedom, . . . for the Orthodox cross."
```

5:19   If other punctuation occurs immediately before a word that is preceded by ellipsis points, that punctuation mark is placed before the word, with the usual intervening space:

> "All this is not exactly in S's tradition . . . ; and it was not, as I recall, your style."

OMISSION FOLLOWING A SENTENCE

5:20   An omission following a sentence is indicated by four dots. The first, placed immediately after the last word, is the period:

> "When a nation is clearly in the wrong, it ought not to be too proud to say so. . . . I have not been enunciating principles which we do not apply in our own case."

If in the original source the sentence preceding the ellipsis ends with a question mark or an exclamation mark, that mark rather than the period is used:

> "How cold it was! . . . No one could function in that climate."

5:21   How much of an omission may be indicated by a mark of terminal punctuation and three dots? Earlier editions of this *Manual* called for the insertion of a full line of ellipsis points to mark the omission of a paragraph or more in a quotation set in block form. But the University of Chicago Press *Manual of Style* now recommends that usage in but a few instances. These are discussed below in paragraphs 5:22, 5:23, and 5:37. In current practice, the period (or other mark of terminal punctuation) and three spaced dots may indicate the omission of (1) the last part of a quoted sentence, or (2) the first part of a quoted sentence, or (3) the last part of one sentence and the first part of the next sentence, or (4) a whole sentence or more, or (5) a whole paragraph or more. But note the following exceptions.

WHEN TO USE A LINE OF
ELLIPSIS POINTS

5:22   In quoting an excerpt of poetry, the omission of one or more complete lines is shown by a full line of ellipsis points,

ductory words forms a functional sentence. In the original matter, the following quotation ended with a semicolon. Since functionally it is a sentence, some writers would place a period before the final quotation mark:

"Part of the historical problem concerns the state of affairs in Spain in the period, and part concerns the state of affairs in the Spanish Netherlands."

5:29   Other reputable opinion maintains that in either of the instances set forth above, when the quoted matter forms only a part of the original sentence, the punctuation should indicate that fact by ending the quotation with the author's mark of punctuation, if there is any, plus three ellipsis points, or with the three points alone, followed by quotation marks:

"Part of the historical problem concerns the state of affairs in Spain in the period, and part concerns the state of affairs in the Spanish Netherlands; . . ."

5:30   Choose one of the schemes set forth in paragraphs 5:28 and 5:29 and follow it consistently throughout your paper.

INCOMPLETE QUOTED EXPRESSIONS

5:31   When a quotation consists of a few words or an incomplete sentence, obviously a fragment from the original, no ellipsis points should be used either before or after the fragment. If, however, an omission occurs within the fragment, it is noted by three ellipsis points:

General Bliss wrote that the president had been "very much impressed" by the South African Jan Smuts's paper which stressed "putting a considerable part of the world under tutelage . . . of the great powers."

OMISSIONS IN FOREIGN-LANGUAGE QUOTATIONS

5:32   Omissions in foreign-language quotations are treated the same as those in English. This is a change from the recommendations made in earlier editions of this *Manual* and is in line with the present practice of the University of Chicago Press as well as other leading publishers.[2]

BLOCK QUOTATIONS

5:33   When a block quotation (par. 5:2) begins with a paragraph in the original matter, it is given paragraph indention of four spaces and the first word is capitalized. Thus with a block quotation indented four spaces from the text, the paragraph indention is eight spaces from the text.

```
Goodenough raises questions that Kraeling does
not raise:

        Primarily why did the artist want to put
    David as the tamer just here? We have seen
    that the original vine or tree growing from
    the vase was changed to make more explicit
    the symbolic and ritualistic implications of
    the vase.
```

5:34   When a quotation begins within the first sentence of a paragraph, whether or not the quotation is syntactically joined to the introductory text, the omission of the first words of the paragraph is shown by three ellipsis dots, the first dot given paragraph indention:

```
We may find statements in talmudic literature which
are relevant to the art, but we must in any case
after assembling the material determine

        . . . what this art means in itself,
    before we begin to apply to it as proof
    texts any possible unrelated statements of
    the Bible or the Talmud.
```

5:35   If a block quotation is introduced in text with quoted fragments interspersed with the words of the writer, the fragments must all have quotation marks at beginning and end. It is not permissible to begin a quotation in text with quotation marks at the beginning, as required, and to continue the quotation in block form, where ending punctua-

[2]If the paper itself is written in a language other than English, the writer should follow the rules of that language in the matter of omissions (as well as in punctuation). Some of these rules are given in the University of Chicago *Manual of Style*, 12th edition.

tion marks are not used. Note the following example of *incorrect usage* in introducing the block quotation:

```
Religion is just "the product of the craving to
know whether these imaginary conceptions have
realities answering to them in some other world
than ours." And Mill continues, "Belief in a
God or Gods
```

```
        and in a life after death becomes the canvas
        which every mind . . . covers with such ideal
        pictures as it can either invent or copy.
```

The writer who is aware of this trap will take care that he does not introduce a quotation in text and complete it in block form. The way out may be as easy as it is here:

```
And Mill continues,
        Belief in a God or Gods and in a life after
        death becomes the canvas which every mind . . .
        covers with such ideal pictures as it can either
        invent or copy.
```

Sometimes the writer must rephrase his text or reconsider the amount to be quoted.

5:36   Two conditions under which a block quotation begins with paragraph indention are considered in paragraphs 5:33 and 5:34. When those conditions are not present, the first line of the block quotation is indented four spaces from the left marginal line, as shown in the example immediately above. Note that the first (partial) paragraph is the only one in a block quotation of more than one paragraph that may be set flush. All the others must be given paragraph indention, whether the quotation begins with the first sentence of the paragraph or at some point within it. If the latter, the paragraph opens with three ellipsis points begun after the four-space paragraph indention, as illustrated in paragraph 5:34.

5:37   If in a quotation of several paragraphs, there is an omission of a full paragraph or more, that omission should be indicated by a period and three ellipsis points at the end of the paragraph preceding the omission. Thus it may be possible that four dots at the end of a paragraph may be followed by three dots at the beginning of the next paragraph, as provided in paragraph 5:36 and illustrated in the last two paragraphs of the following example. This use of two consecutive sets of ellipsis points may occur in a block quotation, but not in a quotation that is run into text.

Recalling as an adult the time in his early youth
when a "new conscience" was forming, Merton writes:

. . . A brand-new conscience was just coming
into existence as an actual, operating function
of a soul. My choices were just about to become
responsible. . . .
. . . since no man ever can, or could, live
by himself and for himself alone, the destinies
of thousands of other people were bound to be
affected, some remotely, but some very directly
and near-at-hand, by my own choices and decisions
and desires, as my own life would also be formed
and modified according to theirs.

5:38 If it is considered desirable—and one can think of instances in which it would be—to quote in block form fragments of prose which are widely scattered in the original source, a full line of ellipsis points may be used between the individual fragments.

INTERPOLATIONS

5:39 It is sometimes advisable for the writer to insert in a quotation a word or more of explanation, or clarification, or correction. All such insertions (interpolations) must be enclosed in square brackets: [ ]. Parentheses may *not* be substituted. Seeing a parenthetic element in a quotation, a reader assumes it was put there by the author of the source quoted. Words enclosed in square brackets indicate that the comment was put there by the person quoting the author. If your typewriter has no brackets, they must be inserted in the copy by hand, in permanent black ink.

5:40 To assure the reader that the faulty logic, error in fact, incorrect word, incorrect spelling, or the like, is in the original matter quoted, the Latin word *sic* ("so"; always underlined) may be placed in brackets after the error:

"When the fog lifted, they were delighted to see
that the country was heavily timbered and emmence
[sic] numbers of fowl flying in every direction."

The use of *sic* should not be overdone. Quotations from
sixteenth-century writing, for example, or from obviously
archaic or illiterate writing, should not be strewn with
*sic*s.

5:41 Interpolations made for purposes of clarification or correction are illustrated in the following:

"But since these masters [Picasso, Braque, Matisse]
appeared to be throwing away, rebelling against
academic training, art teaching has itself been
discredited."

"The recipient of the Nobel Peace Award for 1961
[1960] was Albert John Luthuli."

ITALICS (UNDERLINING)

5:42 Words that are not italicized in the original of the matter
quoted may be italicized (underlined in typing) for emphasis
desired by the writer of the paper. The source of the change
should be indicated to the reader in one of three ways:
(1) By a notation enclosed in square brackets and placed
immediately after the underlined words:

"This man described to me another large river
beyond the Rocky Mountains, the southern branch
[italics mine] of which he directed me to take."

(2) By a parenthetical note following the quotation:

"This man described to me another large river
beyond the Rocky Mountains, the southern branch
of which he directed me to take." (Italics mine.)

(3) By a footnote. Either a footnote or the scheme mentioned in (2) is preferable when italics have been added
at two or more points in a quotation.

6 Footnotes

THE USE OF FOOTNOTES

6:1 Footnotes have four main uses: (*a*) to cite the authority for statements in text—specific facts or opinions as well as exact quotations; (*b*) to make cross-references; (*c*) to make incidental comments upon, to amplify or to qualify textual discussion—in short, to provide a place for material which the writer thinks it worthwhile to include but which he feels would disrupt the flow of thought if introduced into the text; (*d*) to make acknowledgments. Footnotes, then, are of two kinds: *reference* (*a* and *b* above), and *content* (*c* and *d* above). A content footnote may also include one or more references, as will be seen in the examples (par. 6:155). Interpretations and examples of footnote form are given in the following pages.

6:2 Unless it is short and uncomplicated, no table, outline, list, letter, or the like, should be placed in a footnote.

FOOTNOTE NUMBERS

6:3 The place in the text at which a footnote is introduced, whether of the reference or of the content category, should be marked with an arabic numeral. Place the numeral slightly above the line (but never a full space above), and do not put a period after it or embellish it with parentheses, brackets, or slashes. The numeral follows a punctuation mark, if any, except the dash, which it precedes.

6:4 The footnote number should follow the passage to which it refers. If the passage is an exact quotation, the footnote number comes at the end of the quotation, not after the author's name or at the end of the textual matter introducing the quotation.

6:5   Footnote numbers must follow one another in numerical order, beginning with figure one (1). Numbering may start over on each page, or at the beginning of each chapter, or it may run continuously through the entire paper. There are possible complications in using the last two schemes, however, since if it was found that a note had been omitted, or that one should be deleted, it would be necessary to renumber the footnotes from the point of the desired change to the end of the chapter or of the paper. The insertion of a note numbered, for example, "1a" is not permissible, and the omission of a number likewise is not permissible.

POSITION OF FOOTNOTES

6:6   Footnotes should be arranged in numerical order at the foot of the page, and all those to which references are made in the text page must appear on the same page as the references to them.

6:7   Reduction in the number of reference numbers in the text improves the appearance of the page and saves space in the footnote area as well as in typing time. Consider the spotty effect and the waste space resulting from a line or a column of *ibid.*'s. With careful planning, the number of footnotes and their bulk as well can often be considerably reduced without curtailing scholarly responsibilities. Three ways may be mentioned (pars. 6:8–10).

6:8   In a *single* paragraph containing several quotations from one work of the same author, a reference number following the last quotation would permit all the quotations to be cited in one footnote.

6:9   Instead of four reference numbers in the first example below, one number placed after the last name, as in the second example, would allow all four citations to be made in one footnote:

The means by which the traditional Western composers have attempted to . . . communicate with their audiences has been discussed at length . . . by

Eduard Hanslick,[2] Heinrich Schenker,[3] Suzanne Langer,[4]
and Leonard Meyer,[5] to name but a few.

The means by which the traditional Western composers
have attempted to . . . communicate with their
audiences has been discussed at length . . . by
Eduard Hanslick, Heinrich Schenker, Suzanne Langer,
and Leonard Meyer, to name but a few.[2]

The single footnote would then read:

[2]Eduard Hanslick, The Beautiful in Music, trans.
G. Cohen (New York: Novello, Ewer, 1891); Heinrich
Schenker, Der freie Satz, trans. and ed. T. H. Kreuger
(Ann Arbor: University Microfilms, 1960), pub. no.
60–1558; Suzanne Langer, Philosophy in a New Key
(New York: Mentor, 1959); Leonard B. Meyer, Emotion
and Meaning in Music (Chicago: University of Chicago
Press, 1956), and Music, the Arts, and Ideas (Chicago:
University of Chicago Press, 1967).

6:10   Tables, outlines, lists, letters, and the like that are not
immediately relevant to the text are best placed in an
appendix and referred to in the text by a simple footnote:

[1]The member banks and their contributions are
listed in appendix 3.

6:11   If a block quotation (see par. 5:2) contains one or more
footnote references from the original source, the corresponding footnotes should be placed beneath the quotation, not among the footnotes belonging to the paper itself.
An eight-space rule should separate the footnote from the
quotation, and the reference index — whether number or
symbol — and the form of the footnote should follow exactly
the style found in the original material.

They might all have said, along with Bataille
himself:

My tension, in a sense, resembles a great
welling up of laughter, it is not unlike the
burning passions of Sade's heroes, and yet,
it is close to that of the martyrs, or of the
saints.[23]

[23]"Ma tension ressemble, en un sens, à une
folle envie de rire, elle diffère peu des

> passions dont brûlent les héros de Sade, et
> pourtant, elle est proche de celle des martyrs
> ou des saints." <u>Sur Nietzsche</u>, p. 12.

If the writer of the paper adds his own footnote references in a block quotation—to identify persons mentioned, for example, or to translate words or passages in a foreign language—the references are numbered in sequence with the other footnotes in the paper. The corresponding footnotes themselves are placed at the bottom of the page.

6:12   Specific directions for the typing of footnotes and for their correct placing on the page are given in the chapter on typing the paper (pars. 13:26–36).

REFERENCE FOOTNOTES

FIRST FULL REFERENCES

6:13   *Basic style.* The first time a work is mentioned in a footnote,[1] the entry should be in complete form; that is, it should include not only the author's full name, the title of the work, and the specific reference (i.e., volume, if any, and page number), but the facts of publication as well. Once a work has been cited in full, subsequent references to it should be in abbreviated form. These forms are fully discussed and illustrated in paragraphs 6:138–54.

6:14   With some exceptions, such as references to legal, classical, and biblical works, and to certain classes of public documents, and references in scientific papers—all discussed hereafter—footnotes citing a published work the first time are given in the sequence indicated below. Although not every footnote entry will include all the items of information listed, the order should be maintained, regardless of the items omitted.

6:15   For a book, the source of the information, except the page number(s), should be the title page; for a periodical, it should be the cover and the article itself.

[1]Sample footnote references with corresponding bibliographical entries are shown in chapter 8.

6:16 *For a book.* The first, full reference to a book includes:
  Name of author(s) (see pars. 6:19–29)[2]
  Title of book (see pars. 6:30–34)
  Name of editor, compiler, or translator, if any (see pars. 6:35–37)
  Name of author of preface, introduction, or foreword, if any (see par. 6:38)
  Name of series in which book appears, if any, with volume or number in the series (see pars. 6:39–40)
  Number or name of edition, if other than the first (see pars. 6:43–48)
  Total number of volumes, if more than one (see par. 6:49)
  Facts of publication, consisting of
      Place of publication (see pars. 6:51–55)
      Name of publishing agency (see pars. 6:56–65)
      Date of publication (see pars. 6:66–70)
  Volume number, if any (see pars. 6:72–79)
  Page number(s) of the specific citation (see pars. 6:81–84)

6:17 *For an article in a periodical.*[3] The first, full reference to an article in a periodical includes:
  Name of author(s) (see pars. 6:19–29)
  Title of article (see pars. 6:30–34)
  Name of periodical (see pars. 6:30–32)
  Volume number, if any (see pars. 6:32–33, 6:73–78)
  Date of volume or issue (see pars. 6:32–33, 6:74–79)
  Page number(s) (see pars. 6:74, 6:76, 6:81–86)

6:18 Under their separate heads, the items of information listed above for a book and for an article in a periodical are discussed in detail in the following paragraphs.

6:19 *Name of author(s).* Give the name(s) of the author(s) in normal order—Robert John Blank—and follow with a comma. Give the first name and initial of the second name (or first and second names), not initials only, except for

---

[2]The paragraph numbers in parentheses following each item refer to the detailed discussion.
[3]The discussion treats only of articles in journals and magazines. Newspapers are dealt with separately (pars. 6:97–100).

well-known authors who habitually use only the initials of their given names (e.g., T. S. Eliot, D. H. Lawrence, J. B. S. Haldane, W. B. Yeats). For an author whose first names appear on the title pages of some of his works, and initials only on others, footnote references to the latter should give the name as, for example, H[enry] R[obert] Anderson.

6:20   If the title page, or the byline at the head of an article, gives a pseudonym known to be that of a certain author, the real name is used in the footnote and the pseudonym is enclosed in square brackets and placed after it (see example, par. 8:9). Such familiar pseudonyms as Anatole France, George Eliot, and Mark Twain should, however, be used in place of the real name.

6:21   If a pseudonym is indicated as such on the title page, the abbreviation "pseud." is enclosed in parentheses and placed after the name: Helen Delay (pseud.).

6:22   If pseudonymity is not indicated on the title page, but is nevertheless an established fact, the abbreviation "pseud." may be placed in brackets after the name: Helen Delay [pseud.].

6:23   If the title page gives no author's name, or if it designates the work as anonymous, and if in either case the authorship has been definitely established, the author's name, enclosed in square brackets, may be placed before the title: [Henry K. Black]. The use of "Anonymous" in place of the name of an author is not recommended. If the authorship is not reliably established, the footnote reference should begin with the title of the work.

6:24   For a work by two or by three authors, give the full names in normal order, separating the names of the two authors with "and"; of three authors, with commas, the last comma followed by "and":

Walter E. Houghton and G. Robert Stange

Bernard R. Berelson, Paul F. Lazarsfeld, and William N. McPhee

6:25   If a work has more than three authors, it is usual to cite in the footnote (but not in the bibliography), only the name of the author given first on the title page and to follow it with "et al." (*et alii*) or with the English equivalent, "and others." Note that the name of only the first-mentioned author should be given and that whether you choose to follow it with "et al." or with "and others," you should use the same style throughout the paper. No comma comes between the author's name and "et al."

    Gilbert W. King et al.   John Q. Smith and others

    (See example, par. 8:6.)

6:26   For coauthors with the same surname, cite each name in full in the first reference—Sidney Webb and Beatrice Webb, not Sidney and Beatrice Webb. In later references, write Webb and Webb, not the Webbs.

6:27   Even though a title page may include after an author's name a title such as doctor, professor, president, or indicate a scholastic degree or an official position, all such designations should be omitted except in rare instances where one or more of them would have special significance for the subject of the paper.

6:28   The "author" may be a corporate body—a country, state, city, legislative body, institution, society, business firm, committee, or the like. (See example, par. 8:10.)

6:29   Some works—compilations, anthologies—are produced by compilers or editors, whose names appear in place of authors' names and are followed by the abbreviation "ed." (or "eds.") or "comp." (or "comps."):

    Robert E. Kingery and Maurice F. Tauber, eds.

    (See example, par. 8:11.)

6:30   *Title of the work.* Enter the full title of a book as it appears on the title page. Enter the title of an article as it appears at the head of the article, and follow with the name of the periodical, placing a comma between them. Adhere to the peculiarities, if any, of spelling and punctuation within the titles, but capitalize in accordance with the general rule as it applies to the titles of all classes of written works, whether they are published or in manuscript form (see pars. 4:5–12).

6:31   Underline the title of a whole published work, that is, the title of a book and the title of a periodical. Enclose in quotation marks the title of an article in a periodical. Place a comma after the title of a book unless it is followed immediately by parentheses enclosing the facts of publication, in which case the comma is placed after the final parenthesis.

[1]Arthur C. Kirsch, Dryden's Heroic Drama (Princeton, N.J.: Princeton University Press, 1964), p. 15.

6:32   Place no comma between the title of a periodical and the volume number. If the volume number is further identified by a date, the date appears in parentheses.

6:33   A colon, not a comma, separates volume number from page number, but note that when the volume number is followed by a date enclosed in parentheses, the colon comes after the final parenthesis:

[1]Samuel M. Thompson, "The Authority of Law," Ethics 75 (October 1964):16–24.

[2]William W. Crosskey, Politics and the Constitution in the History of the United States, 2 vols. (Chicago: University of Chicago Press, 1953), 1:48.

6:34   Since display headings, both on title pages and at the heads of articles, frequently set a title in two or more lines, and since punctuation is normally omitted at the ends of lines of display headings, it is often necessary to add marks of punctuation to a title as it will appear when written out in text or footnote or bibliography. This need occurs most often in titles composed of a main title and a subtitle. Consider the following example:

The Early Growth of Logic in the Child
Classification and Seriation

Here, as the title is shown on the title page, no punctuation follows *Child*. When it is copied without change from the title page, the title looks like this:

> Wrong: The Early Growth of Logic in the
>   Child Classification and Seriation

Adding a colon after *Child* clarifies the meaning:

> Right: The Early Growth of Logic in the
>   Child: Classification and Seriation

6:35 *Name of editor, translator, or compiler.* If the title page contains in addition to the name of an author that of an editor, translator, or compiler, that name follows the title, being preceded by the appropriate abbreviation: "ed." or "trans." or "comp." In this case the abbreviation stands for "edited by" or "translated by" or "compiled by," and thus is never given in the plural form:

> [1]Edward Chiera, They Wrote on Clay, ed.
> George G. Cameron (Chicago: University of Chicago
> Press, 1938), p. 42.

6:36 A work may have both an editor and a translator as well as an author, and the same person may be both editor and translator:

> [1]Helmut Thielicke, Man in God's World, trans.
> and ed. John W. Doberstein (New York and Evanston,
> Ill.: Harper & Row, 1963), p. 43.
>
> [2]August von Haxthausen, Studies on the Interior
> of Russia, ed. S. Frederick Starr, trans. Eleanore
> L. M. Schmidt (Chicago: University of Chicago Press,
> 1972), p. 47.

6:37 Similar in style is the entry of a work in which the author's name is included in the title. Here the author's name as the first item of information is omitted, although you might properly choose to insert it even though the title page omitted it:

> [1]The Works of Shakespear, ed. Alexander Pope,
> 6 vols. (London: printed for Jacob Tonson in the
> Strand, 1723–25), 2:38.
>
> Or:
>
> [1]Shakespear, The Works of Shakespear, ed.
> Alexander Pope, . . .

Although the foregoing arrangement, which gives the editor's name following the title of the work, is the form of reference most commonly used for this kind of work, it would be permissible in a paper dealing primarily with the work of Pope to give his name first, followed by "ed.":

> [1]Alexander Pope, ed., <u>The Works of Shakespear</u>, 6 vols. (London: printed for Jacob Tonson in the Strand, 1723–25), 2:38.

6:38 *Name of author of preface, foreword, or introduction.* If the title page of a book includes the name of the author of a preface, foreword, or introduction, that name is included in the reference. Note the style of the first of the following references, which is to Hammarskjöld's text:

> [1]Dag Hammarskjöld, <u>Markings</u>, with a Foreword by W. H. Auden (New York: Alfred A. Knopf, 1964), p. 38.

The following reference, however, refers to the Foreword of the book, by W. H. Auden:

> [1]W. H. Auden, Foreword to <u>Markings</u>, by Dag Hammarskjöld (New York: Alfred A. Knopf, 1964), p. ix.

6:39 *Name of series.* Books and pamphlets are sometimes published as parts of named series (e.g., Oxford English Monographs, Yale Studies in Political Science, Monographs of the Society for Research in Child Development), which are sponsored by publishers, institutions — especially universities and graduate schools — governmental agencies, learned societies, commercial and industrial firms, and so on. Although a series bears some resemblance to a periodical publication and to a multivolume work as well, there are important differences stemming from their individual plans of publication — differences that are reflected in the particular style of reference appropriate to each. It may be helpful to describe briefly the three kinds of publications (pars. 6:40–42).

6:40 *Series.* The publication of a series is an ongoing project of its sponsors, whose purpose is the issuance from time to time of books or pamphlets by different writers on topics which may range rather widely over a specific field or discipline or area of interest. Many series are numbered; the citation of a particular work in a numbered series should include the volume number (or issue number) after the name of the series. Note that the volume number here applies to the series and the page number to the book and therefore the citation differs from that for a multivolume work (see par. 6:41). Note also that although the title of the work is underlined, the name of the series is neither underlined nor quoted:

[1]Herbert Jacob, German Administration since Bismarck: Central Authority versus Local Autonomy, Yale Studies in Political Science, vol. 5 (New Haven, Conn.: Yale University Press, 1963), p. 124.

[2]National Industrial Conference Board, Research and Development, Studies in Business Economics, no. 82 (New York: National Industrial Conference Board, 1963), p. 21.

[3]Maximillian E. Novak, Defoe and the Nature of Man, Oxford English Monographs (London: Oxford University Press, 1963), p. 45.

6:41   *Multivolume work.* The publication of a multivolume work falls within limits that are more or less clearly defined in advance. The work consists, or will consist, of a number of volumes related to the same subject. All the volumes may be the work of one author and bear the same title (n. 1); or they may be by one author and have different titles (n. 2); or they may be by different authors and bear different titles, with the entire work carrying an overall title and having a general editor (n. 3).

[1]Paul Tillich, Systematic Theology, 3 vols. (Chicago: University of Chicago Press, 1951–63), 2:48.

[2]Gerald E. Bentley, The Jacobean and Caroline Stage, vols. 1, 2: Dramatic Companies and Players; vols. 3–5: Plays and Playwrights; vol. 6: Theatres; vol. 7: Appendixes to Volume 6 and Indexes; 7 vols. (Oxford: Clarendon Press, 1941–68), 3:28.

[3]Gordon N. Ray, gen. ed., An Introduction to Literature, vol. 1: Reading the Short Story, by Herbert Barrows; vol. 2: The Nature of Drama, by Hubert Hefner; vol. 3: How Does a Poem Mean? by John Ciardi; vol. 4: The Character of Prose, by

Wallace Douglas; 4 vols. (Boston: Houghton Mifflin
Co., 1959), 2:47–48.

(See also par. 6:68.)

6:42   *Periodical.* A periodical is published at stated intervals —
daily, weekly, monthly, quarterly, and so on — the issues
being numbered in succession. In general, each issue of a
magazine or journal is composed of articles by different
authors. References to such articles follow the pattern set
forth in paragraphs 6:31–33. The proper style for citing
articles is not likely to raise any question except when an
entire issue of a publication is devoted to one long paper,
usually by one author. Sometimes such an issue replaces
the more usual multi-article issue, bearing the number of
that issue in the succession of numbers; sometimes it bears
a supplementary number. In either case, its citation raises
a question: Should the citation conform to the style used
for a *whole* publication, or to that used for an article in a
whole publication? The answer lies in the view taken by
the publishers of the periodicals and by the libraries that
a paper occupying a whole issue is published *in* the periodical. Thus it is cited as an article, except that the special
designation shown on the cover of the particular issue is
included in the reference (e.g., supplement, special issue,
etc.):

[1]Elias Folker, "Report on Research in the
Capital Markets," Journal of Finance 39, supplement
(May 1964):15.

6:43   *Edition.* Information concerning the edition is required
if the work cited is other than the first edition. The information is frequently printed on the title page, but it is often
found on the copyright page (the reverse of the title page).
Besides numbered editions, there are named editions, reprint editions, and paperback editions (pars. 6:44–48).

6:44   *Numbered editions.* Although new editions are usually
numbered, they may be designated merely as New Edition,
or New Revised Edition, and so on. Also found are: Second
Edition, Revised; Revised Second Edition; Third Edition,
Revised and Enlarged; Revised Edition in One Volume;
Fourth Edition, Revised by John Doe; and so forth. The

designations should be abbreviated in footnote and bibliographical entries: "new ed."; "new rev. ed."; "2d ed., rev."; "rev. 2d ed."; "3d ed., rev. and enl."; "rev. ed. in 1 vol."; "4th ed., rev. John Doe"; and other variants:

[1]Charles E. Merriam, New Aspects of Politics, 3d ed., enl., with a Foreword by Barry D. Karl (Chicago: University of Chicago Press, 1972), p. 46.

[2]John Wight Duff, A Literary History of Rome from the Origins to the Close of the Golden Age, 3d ed., edited by A. M. Duff (New York: Barnes and Noble, 1964), p. 86. [If "edited by" were not preceded by the edition number, the abbreviation "ed." would be used. See par. 6:35.]

6:45   *Reprint editions.* Works that are out of print are frequently reissued by publishers in special reprint editions. Footnote and bibliographical entries should note the reprint information and give also the date of the original publication and if possible the publisher:

[1]Gunnar Myrdal, Population: A Problem for Democracy (Cambridge: Harvard University Press, 1940; reprint ed., Gloucester, Mass.: Peter Smith, 1956), p. 9.

It is not necessary to note a new printing—e.g., 4th impression—by the original publisher (see par. 6:66).

6:46   *Paperback editions.* Sometimes published at the same time as hardbound editions, sometimes at a later date, many paperback editions of scholarly works are now available. Since the paperback edition is sometimes an abridgment of the hardbound work, the pagination of the two may differ. It is important, therefore, that any references to a paperback edition state that the work is a paperback and give the name of the edition, the publisher, and the date:

[1]George F. Kennan, American Diplomacy, 1900–1950 (Chicago: University of Chicago Press, Phoenix Books, 1970), p. 48.

6:47   If a hardbound edition is used and the work is available in paperback, it may be helpful to your reader to include information on both editions:

[1]George F. Kennan, American Diplomacy, 1900–1950 (Chicago: University of Chicago Press, 1951;

also in paperback edition by the same publisher,
Phoenix Books, 1970), pp. 80–82.

6:48   *Named editions.* Many classics are found in named editions. When they are used in references, they should be
specified:

[1]Blaise Pascal, Pensées and The Provincial
Letters, The Modern Library (New York: Random House,
1941), p. 418.

The title pages of some named editions do not give the name
of the publisher. If only city and date can be given, they
are separated by a comma.

6:49   *Number of volumes.* A reference to a multivolume work
as a whole should include the total number of volumes:

[1]Paul Tillich, Systematic Theology, 3 vols.
(Chicago: University of Chicago Press, 1951–63).

A reference to one of the volumes may be in one of the two
styles discussed in paragraph 6:68.

6:50   *Facts of publication.* As listed in paragraph 6:16, the
facts of publication include the place (city), publisher,
and date. They appear in footnotes as follows:

(London: Hogarth Press, 1964)

These facts are given for printed books, monographs, and
pamphlets, and for published works that are mimeographed,
multigraphed, or otherwise produced by a copy-machine
process (see par. 4:16). But note the following exceptions:

Classical and biblical works	omit	all facts of publication
Legal works and some public documents	usually omit	all but the date
Dictionaries, general encyclopedias, and atlases	omit	all but edition and date
In certain disciplines and in certain fields, the citations	omit	name of publisher

Periodicals, in general	omit	all but the date

6:51 *Place of publication.* If the names of two or more cities appear under the publisher's imprint, the first-named is the location of the editorial offices, and that is normally all that need be given in the reference. But all the names mentioned may be included, as, for example, "Oxford, London, and New York." Do not assume, however, that London and New York may properly be added when Oxford alone appears on the title page.

6:52 If the city is not generally well known, give the state as well, using the standard abbreviation for the state, as "Glencoe, Ill." Identify Cambridge by writing either "Cambridge, England" (never "Engl.") or "Cambridge, Mass." unless the first is followed by "Cambridge University Press" and the second by "Harvard University Press" or "M.I.T. Press."

6:53 For foreign cities, use the English name if there is one: Cologne, not Köln; Munich, not München; Florence, not Firenze; Padua, not Padova; Milan, not Milano; Rome, not Roma; Vienna, not Wien; Prague, not Praha; and so forth.

6:54 If neither the title page nor the copyright page gives the place of publication, write "n.p." (for "no place") as the first item of information on facts of publication. Follow it with a colon if a publisher is given, with a comma if only the date follows.

6:55 The abbreviation "n.p." may also stand for "no publisher." If both place and publisher are missing, "n.p." with the date tells the whole story.

6:56 *Name of publishing agency.*[4] The name of the publisher may be given either in the style used by the company itself or in the accepted abbreviated form as it is given for

---

[4]The broader term, "publishing agency," rather than "publisher," is used here because some of the works are published by societies, institutions of learning, commerce, banking, and the like, which are not publishers per se. The terms are used interchangeably in the text of the section.

American publishers in *Books in Print,* issued annually by R. R. Bowker Co., and for British publishers in *British Books in Print: The Reference Catalogue of Current Literature,* published by J. Whitaker & Sons, London, and distributed in the United States by R. R. Bowker Co.

6:57 Note carefully the spelling and punctuation of publishers' names. There is no comma in Houghton Mifflin Co., for example; but there is a comma in the name of Little, Brown & Co., and in that of Harcourt, Brace & Co., as the firm was formerly known. Hyphens separate the names in McGraw-Hill Book Co. and in Appleton-Century-Crofts. There is a small "m," not a capital "M," in the middle of Macmillan. The name of the New York firm is Macmillan Co., that of the London firm Macmillan & Co.

6:58 Even though you may choose to write publishers' names in full, it is customary to omit an initial "The" and the abbreviation "Inc." or "Ltd." or "S.A."; to use the ampersand (&) in place of "and"; and to abbreviate "Company" to "Co." and "Brother" or "Brothers" to "Bro." or "Bros." Whatever the style chosen, it must be used consistently throughout the paper.

6:59 If the title page indicates that a work was copublished, the reference should give both publishers:

```
(New York: Alfred A. Knopf and Viking Press, 1966)
(Boston: Ginn & Co., 1964; Montreal: Round Press,
1964)
```

6:60 The title page of a book issued by a subsidiary of a publisher gives both names, and references to such a book should include both:

```
(Cambridge: Harvard University Press, Belknap
Press, 1965)
```

6:61 If a work was published for an institution, society, or the like, and their name appears on the title page together with the publisher's name, the references should include both names:

```
(New York: Columbia University Press for the
American Geographical Society, 1947)
```

6:62   If a work has been reprinted at a date later than that of its original publication, the fact will usually be noted on the entry card for the work in the library card catalog. Such information is especially useful for locating some hard-to-find old works. (See par. 6:45 for the style of reference used in citing a reprint edition.)

6:63   Do not substitute the present name of a publishing firm for that shown on the title page of the work being cited.

6:64   Do not translate parts of the names of foreign publishers, even when you have anglicized the name of the city (par. 6:53). Do not, for example, change "Compagnie" or "Cie.," to "Company" or "Co."; or "et Frère," to "and Brother" or "and Bro."

6:65   Certain disciplines and certain fields, in accord with long-established practice, commonly omit names of publishers from their references. Thus, only place and date of publication appear, as, for example, "New York, 1970." Note that when only two facts of publication are given, they are separated with a comma.

6:66   *Date of publication.* The date usually appears on the title page, either with the publisher's imprint or overleaf in the copyright data. There may be more than one copyright date; if so, the last is the one under which the work in hand was issued. But there may also be one or more dates shown in addition to the date of copyright. Since those refer to *reprintings,* or new impressions, not new editions, they should be disregarded. The date of copyright is the one to use in your reference—unless a different date appears with the publisher's imprint on the title page; the latter would then be the one to use. If no date is shown any place, write "n.d." (for "no date"):

(New York: Grosset & Dunlap, n.d.)

6:67   If, however, the date has been established by means other than the title page or copyright page, place the date in square brackets. The entry for the work in the card catalog of the library often carries the date of publication when the title page omits it. When the date has been discovered through the efforts of the library, it will be shown on the entry card in square brackets. In a footnote it is given thus:

```
(New York: Grosset & Dunlap, [1931])
```

6:68   It has been noted that a first reference to a multivolume work includes the total number of volumes (par. 6:49) together with the facts of publication. If the individual volumes have been issued in different years, the reference must indicate that fact by a footnote in one of the following forms:

```
    1Paul Tillich, Systematic Theology, 3 vols.
(Chicago: University of Chicago Press, 1951–63),
2:182.

    2Paul Tillich, Systematic Theology, 3 vols.
(Chicago: University of Chicago Press, 1951–63),
2 (1957):182.
```

The style of the second reference should be used when the writer desires to show the date of publication of the specific volume.

6:69   Since all the volumes of the multivolume work mentioned in the following note were published in one year, there is no need to repeat the publication date of the volume cited:

```
    3Gordon N. Ray, gen. ed., An Introduction to
Literature, 4 vols. (Boston: Houghton Mifflin Co.,
1959), vol. 2: The Nature of Drama, by Hubert Hefner,
pp. 47–49.
```

(Here "vol." and "pp." are used because they do not refer to the same title: "vol. 2" means the second volume of *An Introduction to Literature* and "pp. 47–49" refers to that volume itself, *The Nature of Drama*.)

6:70   When the publication of a multivolume work is not complete, give the date when publication began and follow with a dash: 1968–

6:71   References to periodicals normally omit place and publisher (newspaper names do, however, include place; see par. 6:97), except that for foreign periodicals of limited circulation, and titles that are identical or similar to periodicals published elsewhere, the place of publication should be included:

> [1]Jack Fishman, "Un grand homme dans son intimité: Churchill," Historia (Paris), no. 220 (November 1964), pp. 684–94.

6:72 *Volume number.* Reference to a work of more than one volume must give the volume number as well as the page(s). If the reference is the first to the work, include the facts of publication.

6:73 As shown in examples on previous pages, volume numbers are expressed in arabic numerals rather than roman, which the earlier editions of this *Manual* have specified. The change has been made to accord with the recommendation of the University of Chicago Press *Manual of Style,* 12th edition. In scientific, technical, and legal writing, the more convenient arabic numerals replaced the roman some years ago, and gradually in other fields as well the arabic numerals have been adopted. Volume numbers of books and periodicals, then, should be given in arabic numerals, regardless of whether they are expressed in roman or in arabic in the works cited.

6:74 This *Manual* has always recommended the omission of the abbreviations "vol." and "p." or "pp." when a reference cites both volume and page(s) of the same work. Now if both are shown in arabic numerals and no identifying abbreviations are used, some way of distinguishing volume from page is clearly necessary. The scheme that is recommended by *A Manual of Style* is followed in this thesis manual, that is, to give volume number first and page number second and to separate them with a colon:

> [1]Don Swanson, "Dialogue with a Catalogue," Library Quarterly 34 (December 1963):113–25.

When the volume number is followed directly by a parenthesis, as it is in the example, the colon comes after the parenthesis rather than before. (See also par. 6:68.)

6:75 References to magazines and journals that are issued weekly, monthly, bimonthly, quarterly, and so on, should give the volume number in arabic numerals immediately after the title of the publication (see example in par. 6:74). Ordinarily, the date — month and year — is enclosed in parentheses and placed immediately after the volume number. Note that there is no mark of punctuation between the title of the publication and the volume number, and none between month and year.

6:76   The number of the issue need not be given, unless the periodical is one that is numbered *only by issue*, not by volume and issue. The reference to such a periodical should give the issue number followed by the year date in parentheses:

> [1]Konrad Lorenz, "The Wisdom of Darwin," Midway, no. 22 (1965), p. 48.

Note that when issue number rather than volume is given, a comma separates it from the title of the periodical; also that page number is preceded by the abbreviation "p." or "pp."

6:77   Some periodicals publish volumes in successive series, each beginning with volume 1. In some cases the successive series are numbered; in some they are lettered; and in some they are designated as "Old Series" or "New Series," abbreviated as "o.s." and "n.s.":

> [1]J. Durbin, "Estimation of Parameters in Time Series Regression Models," Journal of the Royal Statistical Society, ser. B, 22 (January 1960):139–53.

6:78   Magazines of general interest, even though they may carry volume numbers, are best identified by date alone. The date then takes the place of the volume number and is not enclosed in parentheses:

> [1]Barbara W. Tuchman, "If Asia Were Clay in the Hands of the West," Atlantic, September 1970, pp. 68–84.

6:79   Daily newspapers and weekly magazines are also identified by date alone:

> [1]Palo Alto (Calif.) Times, 19 November 1970.

Note also paragraphs 6:97–100 "Newspapers."

²Franklin D. Murphy, "Yardsticks for a New
Era," Saturday Review, 21 November 1970, pp. 23–25.

6:80   *Forthcoming work.* If a writer finds it desirable to mention
a work that has been accepted for publication but is not
yet published, he may do so in the following style for a
book:

¹Marshall Hodgson, The Venture of Islam
(Chicago: University of Chicago Press, forthcoming).

And for a journal article:

²Robert D. Hume, "Theory of Comedy in the
Restoration," Modern Philology, forthcoming.

6:81   *Page number(s).* Refer to a single page as, for example,
"p. 60." Refer to inclusive page numbers in accordance
with the scheme set forth in paragraph 2:52.

6:82   Use exact inclusive page numbers in preference to such
designations as "pp. 80 f." (p. 80 and following page) or
"pp. 82, 83 ff." (pp. 82, 83, and following pages). Since
"f." refers to only a single page immediately following
the number given, the exact pages should be cited: "pp.
80–81." Similarly, avoid using "pp. 82, 83 ff.," by giving
inclusive pages, "pp. 82–85," for example.

6:83   Although inclusive page numbers are desirable in referring to an article as a whole, they should not be given when
an article begins in the front of a magazine and skips to
the back. In this case inclusive page numbers are meaning-
less and the first page number alone should be cited.

6:84   The word "passim" ("here and there") should be used
with discretion. Employ it only in referring to information
scattered over a considerable stretch of text, or throughout
a chapter or other long section. Give the inclusive page
numbers or the chapter number and place "passim" at
the end of the reference:

Haxthausen, Studies on the Interior of Russia,
chap. 9 passim.

Kennan, American Diplomacy, pp. 80–85 passim, 92,
105.

Note that passim is a whole word, not an abbreviation, and that it is not underlined.

6:85   *Omission of abbreviations "vol." and "p."* In a reference that includes both a volume and a page number, the abbreviations "vol." and "p." or "pp." are usually omitted (see par. 6:74). In some kinds of references, however, these abbreviations are needed. For example, in the following reference, the volume number is that of the series, not that of the particular work. The abbreviations should be used:

[1]Leonard L. Watkins, Commercial Banking Reform in the United States, Michigan Business Studies, vol. 8, no. 5 (Ann Arbor: University of Michigan, 1938), p. 464.

And in the following reference, the citation of the title and facts of publication of the particular volume requires the fuller treatment:

[1]Gabriel Marcel, The Mystery of Being, vol. 2: Faith and Reality (Chicago: Henry Regnery Co., 1960), pp. 19–20.

(See also the example in par. 6:69.)

6:86   When in addition to volume and page another division of a work is necessary to determine the page reference, that division must be appropriately designated even though the abbreviations "vol." and "p." are omitted:

[1]Donald Lach, Asia in the Making of Europe (Chicago: University of Chicago Press, 1965–), 2, bk. 1:165.

6:87   *Numerals used for other parts of works.* The use of arabic rather than roman numerals to indicate volume numbers is noted in paragraph 6:73. But it is not volume numbers only that are now shown in arabic numerals, but (with some few exceptions) all the divisions of a written work: parts, volumes, books, chapters, pages; acts and scenes of a play; lines and stanzas of a poem; columns of a tabulation; plates, figures, tables, maps; and so on. There are three exceptions: (1) Reference to a book's preliminary pages which are numbered with small roman numerals should use the same style of numeral. (2) References to divisions of public documents or manuscript materials should follow the numbering style of the source. (3) Citation of a collection of inscriptions, papyri, or ostraca that is divided into volumes should use roman numerals for the volume numbers (par. 6:113).

SPLIT REFERENCES

6:88   If at the first reference to a work the author's full name is brought into the text close to the footnote number, it may be omitted from the note. Later in the text, the appearance of only the author's surname permits its omission from the footnote. And similarly, if both the name of the author and the title of the work are given in the text, they may be omitted from the footnote, which then would consist of the facts of publication (if it is the first reference to the work) plus the page number(s), or volume and page(s), if appropriate.

ABBREVIATIONS IN FOOTNOTES, BIBLIOGRAPHIES, AND SO ON

USE OF ABBREVIATIONS

6:89   It was pointed out earlier (par. 2:1) that except in scientific and technical writing, few abbreviations are permissible in text, but that in footnote and bibliographical entries, in tabular matter, and in some kinds of illustrative matter, abbreviations are normally preferred to complete words. Listed below are some abbreviations commonly found in these places. In using them, note the following:

6:90   An abbreviation designating a part of a written work (vol., pt., chap., etc.) should never be used unless it is followed or preceded by a number (vol. 2, pt. 1, chap. 10, pp. 9–11, 4 vols., etc.). When used without numbers these words should be spelled out.

6:91   Of the abbreviations in the following list only "MS" is capitalized at all times, but each abbreviation should begin with a capital when it is the first word of a footnote and whenever the usual rules for capitalization apply.

6:92 The word *sic* is underlined, but not the Latin abbreviations commonly used in footnotes, bibliographies, tabular matter, and so on:

LIST OF ABBREVIATIONS

6:93
```
app., appendix
art., article (plural, arts.)
b., born
bk., book (plural, bks.)
c., copyright
ca., circa, about, approximately
cf., confer, compare (Note that confer is the Latin
     word for "compare"; cf. must not be used as the
     abbreviation for the English "confer," nor
     should cf. be used to mean "see.")
ch., chapter, in legal references only
chap., chapter (plural, chaps.)
col., column (plural, cols.)
comp., compiler (plural, comps.); compiled by
dept., department (plural, depts.)
d., died
div., division (plural, divs.)
e.g., exempli gratia, for example
ed., edition; edited by; editor (plural, eds.)
et al., et alii, and others
et seq., et sequens, and the following
etc., et cetera, and so forth
fig., figure (plural, figs.)'
ibid., ibidem, in the same place
id., idem, the same (used to refer to persons,
     except in law citations; not to be confused
     with ibid.)
infra, below
l.(ell), line (plural, ll.) (Not recommended because
     the abbreviation might be mistaken for "one"
     and the plural for "eleven.")
loc. cit., loco citato, in the place cited
MS, manuscript (plural, MSS)
n., note, footnote (plural, nn.)
n.d., no date
n.p., no place; no publisher
no., number (plural, nos.)
n.s., new series
op. cit., opere citato, in the work cited
o.s., old series
```

```
p., page (plural, pp.)
par., paragraph (plural, pars.)
passim, here and there
pt., part (plural, pts.)
q.v., quod vide, which see
sc., scene
sec., section (plural, secs.)
sic, so, thus
supp., supplement (plural, supps.)
supra, above
s.v., sub verbo, sub voce, under the word
trans., translator; translated by
v., verse (plural, vv.)
viz., videlicet, namely
vol., volume (plural, vols.)
vs., versus, against (v. in law references)
```

ABBREVIATIONS OF TITLES

6:94   Titles of journals, dictionaries, and other sources used frequently in a paper may be abbreviated by the initials of the words of their names, without spaces or periods between the letters. Such abbreviations are permissible in footnote but not in bibliographical entries:

```
AHR, American Historical Review
NRF, Nouvelle Revue Française
DNB, Dictionary of National Biography
OED, Oxford English Dictionary
```

Journals that have initials as actual titles should be so cited in both footnotes and bibliographies.

```
PMLA    MLN    ELH
```

6:95   Also, it is permissible for a writer who must refer frequently to the same work to devise an abbreviation to be used after the first full reference:

```
Christopher Addison, Four and a Half Years, 2 vols.
(London: Hutchinson & Co., 1934), 1:35 (hereafter
cited as Addison, Diary).
```

See also par. 6:154.

CITATION TAKEN FROM A
SECONDARY SOURCE

6:96   In citing the work of one author as found in that of another, both the work in which the reference was found (secondary source) and the title of the work mentioned therein must be given in the reference. In general, the style illustrated in footnote 1 should be followed, but if it is more significant for the purposes of the paper to emphasize Hulbert's citing of the *Jesuit Relations*, the style of the second footnote should be used:

> [1]Jesuit Relations and Allied Documents, vol. 59, n. 41, quoted in [or "cited by"] Archer Butler Hulbert, Portage Paths (Cleveland: Arthur H. Clark, 1903), p. 181.

> [2]Archer Butler Hulbert, Portage Paths (Cleveland: Arthur H. Clark, 1903), p. 181, quoting [or "citing"] Jesuit Relations and Allied Documents, vol. 59, n. 41.

SPECIAL FORMS

NEWSPAPERS

6:97   For reference to a newspaper, the name of the paper and the date are usually sufficient; but many large metropolitan papers—especially Sunday editions—are made up in sections that are separately paginated. For these, section number (or letter) and page number must be given. It is convenient for the reader if the title of the article and the author, if any, are included in the reference:

> "Amazing Amazon Region," New York Times, 12 January 1969, sec. 4, p. E11.

If the name of the newspaper does not include the name of the city, place it before the newspaper title and underline both. If the city is not well known, give the name of the state in parentheses:

> Menlo Park (Calif.) Recorder

If the name of the city is the same as that of another, well-known city, give after it the name of the state in parentheses:

Richmond (Ind.) Palladium, 18 December 1970, p. 1.

6:98 For foreign newspapers in which the city of publication does not form a part of the title, the name of the city should be given in parentheses after the title:

Times (London)	But:	Frankfurter Zeitung
Le Monde (Paris)		Manchester Guardian

6:99 The city of publication need not be given for such well-known newspapers as the *Christian Science Monitor,* the *Wall Street Journal,* and the *National Observer.*

6:100 An initial "The" in English language newspaper titles is omitted, but its equivalent in a foreign language is retained: thus, *Times* (London), but *Le Monde* (Paris). This practice holds for footnote and bibliographical entries, but when a newspaper (or journal or magazine) title appears in the text, "the" may precede if the syntax requires it, but it is not treated as part of the title:

The Sunday edition of the San Francisco Examiner includes an excellent section on entertainment.

The New York Times gives superior coverage to foreign news.

He prefers New York Times editorials to those of any other newspaper.

ARTICLES IN ENCYCLOPEDIAS AND DICTIONARIES

6:101 In citing alphabetically arranged reference works such as encyclopedias and dictionaries, it is best to give the title of the article preceded by "s.v." (*sub verbo,* "under the word") rather than volume and page numbers. Place of publication, publisher's name, and in certain cases the date, are omitted from citations of most reference works. The edition, unless it is the first, is normally mentioned. But here just a word is in order concerning the policy of "continuous revision" under which the major encyclopedias have operated for some years. The number of the edition is not mentioned on their title pages, and the date of publication thus becomes the means of identification. When the title page gives the number of the edition, the reference should include it (n. 1 below); when it does not mention the edition, identify the particular work by date of publication (n. 2). In referring to a signed article, the name of the author may be included. If only the author's initials appear beneath the article, the list of authors in the front matter of the work may provide the name:

[1]Encyclopaedia Britannica, 11th ed., s.v. "Blake, William," by J. W. Comyns-Carr.

[2]Encyclopedia Americana, 1963 ed., s.v. "Sitting Bull."

[3]Columbia Encyclopedia, 3d ed., s.v. "Cano, Juan Sebastián del."

[4]Webster's Geographical Dictionary, rev. ed. (1964), s.v. "Dominican Republic."

NOVELS

6:102 Novels are best referred to by chapter (or by part or book as well as chapter), since many appear in various editions differently paginated:

[1]Joseph Conrad, Heart of Darkness (New York: Doubleday, Page & Co., 1903), chap. 3.

References to recent novels may cite page numbers, but be sure to include the facts of publication (see pars. 6:50–71).

[2]John Cheever, Bullett Park (New York: Alfred A. Knopf, 1969), p. 139.

PLAYS AND LONG POEMS

6:103 References to modern plays follow the style used for books, except that act, scene, and line numbers are given instead of pages:

[1]Louis O. Coxe and Robert Chapman, Billy Budd (Princeton: Princeton University Press, 1951), act 1, sc. 2, line 83.

6:104 For English classics, both plays and long poems, the style of reference may be that used for Greek and Latin classical works (see pars. 6:106–14). If the work is recognized as that of a widely known author, the author's name is frequently omitted; the title is underlined, whether the work is published as a separate volume or as part of a collection, and the facts of publication are seldom given. Among the works so treated are the plays of Shakespeare and of Jonson and such long poems as *The Faerie Queene, Paradise Lost, The Ring and the Book.*

Romeo and Juliet 3. 2. 1–30
          or:
Romeo and Juliet, act 3, sc. 2, lines 1–30

Paradise Lost 1. 83–86
          or:
Paradise Lost, bk. 1, lines 83–86

SHORT POEMS

6:105   Short poems, which most often are published in collections, show the title placed between quotation marks and the name of the collection underlined. Stanza and lines are designated:

Francis Thompson, "The Hound of Heaven," in The Oxford Book of Modern Verse (New York: Oxford University Press, 1937), stanza 3, lines 11–21.

GREEK AND LATIN CLASSICAL WORKS

6:106   References to classical works use abbreviations extensively for: author's name; title of the work; collections of inscriptions, papyri, ostraca, and so on; and for the titles of well-known periodical publications and other reference tools. For a list of accepted abbreviations, the *Oxford Classical Dictionary* should be consulted. It is recommended, however, that such abbreviations not be used except in papers on predominantly classical topics. Sample footnotes appear in paragraph 6:114 below.

6:107   Titles of individual works, collections, and periodicals are underlined, whether they are given in full or abbreviated. In Greek and Latin titles, only the first word, proper nouns, and proper adjectives are capitalized.

6:108   The different levels of division of a work (book, part, section, chapter, lines, etc.) are indicated with *arabic* numerals. (This is a change from the style recommended in earlier editions of this *Manual,* which assigned small roman numerals to books.) When designated by number only, the different levels are separated with periods:

Stat. Silv. 1. 3. 32

In a succession of references to the same level, commas separate the several references:

Ovid Met. 1. 240, 242

A hyphen separates continuing numbers (see par. 6:114, n. 1). If for the sake of clarity, identifying abbreviations are used before the numbers, the several divisions are separated with commas, not periods (bk. 2, sec. 4).

6:109   There is no punctuation between the author's name and the title of the work, and none between the title of the work and the first reference unless the reference is preceded by an identifying abbreviation, in which case a comma intervenes.

6:110   In general, the facts of publication are omitted, but the name of the edition may be given after the title (par. 6:114, n. 4), and it *must be given* if the reference is made to page numbers rather than to book, chapter, and so on.

6:111   The number of an edition, other than the first, is indicated by a superior number placed either after the title or after the volume number if the reference includes volume number (par. 6:114, nn. 7, 8).

6:112   A superior letter or figure placed immediately after a number referring to a division of a work indicates a subdivision (par. 6:114, n. 9). If preferred, the letters may be placed on the line, and either capital or small letters may be used, the choice depending upon usage in the source cited.

6:113   Despite the preference indicated in this *Manual* for arabic numerals rather than roman for volume numbers (see par. 6:87), references to collections of inscriptions, papyri, ostraca, and so forth, should continue to express volume numbers in capital roman numerals. After the volume number comes the document number, followed by numbers indicating the remaining divisions to which reference is made. Note that a comma separates title from volume number, and a comma also separates volume number from document number, after which periods separate the remaining divisions (see par. 6:114, n. 6).

6:114 The following examples illustrate points discussed in paragraphs 6:106–13:

[1]Homer <u>Odyssey</u> 9. 266–71.

    <u>or</u>:

[2]Hom. <u>Od</u>. 9. 266–71.

[3]Cicero <u>De officiis</u> 2. 133, 140.

[4]Horace <u>Satires, Epistles and Ars poetica</u>, Loeb Classical Library, p. 12.

[5]H. Musurillo <u>TAPA</u> 93 (1926): 231.

[6]<u>IG Rom.</u>, III, 739. 9. 10, 17. [This refers to <u>Inscriptiones Graecae ad res Romanas pertinentes</u>, vol. III, document 739, section 9, lines 10 and 17.]

[7]E. Meyer <u>Kleine Schriften</u> 1^2 (Halle, 1924), 382.

[8]Stolz–Schmalz <u>Lat. Gram.</u>[5] (rev. Leumann–Hofmann; Munich, 1928), pp. 490–91.

[9]Aristotle <u>Poetics</u> 20. 1456^b20. 34–35.

[10]<u>POxy</u>. 1485. [POxy. = Oxyrhynchus Papyri. The number cited is that of the document number; there is no volume number.]

MEDIEVAL WORKS

6:115 References to medieval works may be in the same style as that used for Greek and Latin classical works:

[1]Irenaeus <u>Against Heresies</u> 1. 8. 3.

[2]John of the Cross <u>Ascent of Mount Carmel</u> (trans. E. Allison Peers) 2. 20. 5.

[3]<u>Beowulf</u>, lines 2401–7. [When the specific part is named, a comma separates title from reference.]

6:116   Exact references to the Bible and the Apocrypha use abbreviations for the books both in text and in footnotes. Chapter and verse, separated with a colon, are both indicated with arabic numerals. The King James version is assumed unless another is mentioned. There is no underlining:

> [1]Psalm 103:6–14.
>
> [2]1 Cor. 13:1–13 (NEB). [NEB = New English Bible.]

Non-Christian sacred scriptures are referred to in the same manner as Christian.

6:117   The title of a radio or television show is quoted, following the name of the station or of the broadcasting network given in abbreviation. If a specific program is referred to, the date is included; and if it is particularly significant for the textual discussion, more information may be given:

> [1]KQED, "How Do Your Children Grow?"
>
> [2]KPFA, "At Issue," 22 December 1970.
>
> [3]CBS, "Twentieth Century," 28 October 1962, "I Remember: Dag Hammarskjöld," Walter Cronkite.

6:118   Much valuable written material, both of historical and of temporary interest, is preserved in microform. A considerable amount of this material has seen earlier publication in the form of a book or a magazine or a newspaper that could be held in the hand; much also is published only in microform. References to micropublications that are republications of earlier published material should give the relevant facts of the original publication—if available—plus the facts concerning the micropublisher and the publication order number. The titles should be underlined or enclosed in quotation marks as may be suitable for the type of work cited (see pars. 4:16–29). References to works published only in microform should give the facts of publication for the micropublisher and the publication order number. Titles should be underlined:

¹Godwin C. Chu and Wilbur Schramm, Learning from Television: What the Research Says (Bethesda, Md.: ERIC Document Reproduction Service, ED 014 900, 1967).

²Paul Tillich, The Interpretation of History (New York: Charles Scribner's Sons, 1936; Ann Arbor, Mich.: University Microfilms, OP 2783, n.d.).

³U.S., Congress, House, Committee on Interstate and Foreign Commerce, Passenger Train Service, Hearings before the Subcommittee on Transportation and Aeronautics on H.R. 17849 and S. 3706, 91st Cong., 2d sess., 1970 (Washington, D.C.: Congressional Information Service, 500 Montgomery Bldg., CIS H501–33, 1970).

MANUSCRIPT COLLECTIONS

6:119   References to manuscript collections give as a minimum the name of the city in which the depository is located, the name of the depository, and the name or number (or both) of the collection. When a specific document is cited, it is best to mention it first and to include the pertinent facts. If the document has a title, it is in quotation marks; if there is a general designation, such as *diary, letter, telegram, memorandum,* the word is capitalized but not in quotation marks or underlined. Note the difference between the order of the items in a footnote that mentions a specific document and one that does not. (The same collection is used for both examples.)

¹Gen. Joseph C. Castner, "Report to the War Department, 17 January 1927," Modern Military Records Division, Record Group 94, National Archives, Washington, D.C.

²Washington, D.C., National Archives, Modern Military Records Division, Record Group 94.

³Stanley K. Hornbeck, Memorandum on Clarence Gauss, 8 May 1942, Hornbeck Papers, File "Gauss," Hoover Library, Stanford, California.

Do not use the word "letter" if the reference gives names of sender and recipient and date of communication:

[4]Frank Vanderlip to Robert Lansing, 2 September 1915, Frank Vanderlip Papers, Columbia University Library, New York.

MISCELLANEOUS UNPUBLISHED MATERIALS

6:120 Because of their variety, manuscript materials are cited in different forms. If the material has a title, that title is placed within quotation marks, following the name of the sponsoring organization or of the author, if any. If there is a descriptive title, it is not in quotation marks. Mention of the nature of the material follows the title, and although exact location (such as page numbers) can seldom be given, the citation should, if possible, include information which would permit the material to be found. The information given about a personal letter may be much or little, depending upon its value as source material (see nn. 1 and 2).

[1]John Blank, personal letter.

[2]Alan Cranston, California State Controller, to Maurice Sexton, Sacramento, 22 October 1962, Personal Files of Maurice Sexton, Modesto, California.

[3]Morristown (Kansas) Orphan's Home, Minutes of Meetings of the Board of Managers, Meeting of 6 May 1930.

[4]Sidney E. Mead, "Some Eternal Greatness," sermon preached at the Rockefeller Chapel, University of Chicago, 31 July 1960.

[5]O. C. Phillips, Jr., "The Influence of Ovid on Lucan's Bellum civile" (Ph.D. dissertation, University of Chicago, 1962), p. 14.

INTERVIEWS

6:121 References to interviews include the name of the person or the group interviewed, the place, and the date.

[1]A. A. Wyler, interview held during meeting of the American Astronomical Society, Pasadena, California, June 1964.

²Farmers' State Bank, Barrett, Nebraska,
interviews with a selected list of depositors,
August 1960.

LEGAL CITATIONS

6:122   Law publications use a style of citation very different
from that in other fields. Space permits no more than a
brief treatment of legal citations here, and the materials
chosen for illustration are, therefore, those which it is
thought may be most useful to the student. The Harvard
Law Review Association publishes a detailed guide—*A
Uniform System of Citation* (11th ed., 1967). The style of
reference here set forth follows that guide in most re-
spects; where it differs, the changes are due largely to the
fact that this *Manual* is addressed principally to students
using a typewriter rather than to those preparing copy for
printing.

6:123   A conspicuous feature of legal reference usage is that of
abbreviations—for names of periodicals and law reports,
courts, organs of government, besides those commonly
used in footnotes generally. (*A Uniform System* . . . contains a number of lists of such abbreviations.)

6:124   The styles of reference given in the examples in this section are those appropriate for footnotes. In the text, and
in textual matter in footnotes, names of cases and titles of
all publications of whatever kind—books, periodicals,
reports, documents, hearings—are underlined. Materials
such as periodical titles, which are abbreviated in footnotes,
are spelled out in all textual matter.

6:125   Papers on topics that are predominantly legal should employ the style of reference discussed in this section, but
when papers in other fields refer to books and periodicals
in the field of law, as, for example, is frequently done in
the social sciences, the references to legal works should
be adapted to that of the topical field in order to preserve
a uniform style.

6:126   A paper in the field of law may have occasion to refer to
government documents other than those mentioned above.

In such case, the discussion and examples in chapter 9 may be useful. The forms of citation listed there would require change to legal style, as set forth in this section.

6:127   *Court cases.* Citations of court cases give the name of the case, volume number, name of law report(s), page number, and year date, in that order. For decisions that appear in both an official and an unofficial report, it is proper to cite both, the official report being mentioned first (n. 1). Some early reports are named for court reporters (the names of a few are abbreviated, as "Wall." for "Wallace" in n. 2 below). For a reporter of the United States Supreme Court, "U.S." should appear after the name (n. 2); for a state reporter, the state abbreviation. If "ex parte," "ex rel.," or "in re" forms a part of the case name, that expression is underlined; otherwise there is no underlining in the citation (n. 3).

6:128   The court that decided the case must be indicated in the citation. In many instances the name of the report identifies the court, and it is assumed to be the highest in the jurisdiction (n. 4). But most unofficial reports, and all those named for a reporter, do not of themselves indicate the jurisdiction, and both the jurisdiction and the name of the court must be added (n. 5). However, for a case cited to a named reporter, if the court that rendered the decision is the highest of the jurisdiction, only the jurisdiction is mentioned (n. 6). Reference to a case decided by a United States court of appeals must indicate the circuit number (n. 7).

[1]King v. Order of United Commercial Travellers, 333 U.S. 153, 68 Sup. Ct. 488, 92 L. Ed. 608 (1948).

[2]Collector v. Day, 11 Wall. (U.S.), 113 (1870).

[3]<u>Ex parte</u> Mahone, 30 Ala. 49 (1847).

[4]How v. State, 9 Mo. 690 (1846).

[5]Leary v. Friedenthal, 299 S.W. 2d 563 (Mo. Ct. App. 1957).

[6]Morse v. Kieran, 3 Rawle 325 (Pa. 1832).

⁷United States v. Eldridge, 302 F. 2d 463
(4th Cir. 1962).

6:129   For English court cases the pattern of citation follows in
general that of court cases in the United States (n. 8).
Although normally the date is given at the end of the citation, for law reports beginning in 1891 and for the *All
England Reports*, the date is placed in brackets preceding
the series volume and page notation (n. 9). Both the brack-
eted date (of publication) and the volume number are necessary inasmuch as each series is renumbered yearly (nn.
9, 10). In the case of a *decision date* differing in year from
the publication date, the decision date is added at the end
of the citation (n. 10).

⁸Comber v. Jones, 3 Bos. & Pull. 114, 127
Eng. Rep. 62 (C.P. 1802).

⁹Fyfe v. Garden [1946], 1 All E.R. 366 (H.L.).

¹⁰Lemon v. Lardeur [1947], 2 All E.R. 329
(C.A. 1946).

6:130   *Statutory materials.* Constitutions are cited to article and
section (and clause, if relevant) (n. 11). An amendment
to the United States Constitution should be given by number, followed by notation of the section (n. 12). If in a
reference to a portion of a state constitution, that portion
has been significantly amended since the time for which it
is cited, or if it is no longer in force, the date of adoption
of the portion cited is given (n. 14).

¹¹U.S. Const. art. I, sec. 5.

¹²U.S. Const. amend. XIV, sec. 2.

¹³Ill. Const. art. 5, sec. 2.

¹⁴N.Y. Const. art 2, sec. 6 (1894).

6:131   Before enactment, congressional bills and resolutions are
cited:

¹⁵H. R. 11818, 89th Cong., 1st sess., sec. 301(a)
(1965).

¹⁶S. Res. 218, 83d Cong., 2d sess. (1954).

6:132   After passage, bills and joint and concurrent resolutions are cited as statutes. They reach the *U.S. Code* in steps, as time for publication permits, appearing in the *Congressional Record* (n. 17) before publication in the *Statutes at Large* (n. 18), and often in the *U.S. Code Annotated* before the *Code*. After publication in the *Code*, statutes should be cited to the *Code* alone or, as a matter of convenience for the reader, both to the *Statutes* and the *Code* (n. 19). Many statutes are cited by popular name as well as official name (n. 19). Untitled acts are cited as in note 20.

[17]S. Con. Res. 21, 83d Cong., 2d sess., 100 Cong. Rec. 2929 (1954).

[18]Clayton Act, 64 Stat. 1125 (1950).

[19]Labor Management Relations Act (Taft–Hartley Act), sec. 301(a), 61 Stat. 156 (1947), 29 U.S.C., sec. 185(a) (1952). [References to the U.S. Code are always to sections, not pages.]

[20]Act of July 23, 1947, ch. 302, 61 Stat. 413.

6:133   Citations of state laws follow the pattern of federal laws:

[21]Corporate Securities Law, Cal. Corp. Code, secs. 25000–26104.

6:134   English statutes are cited by name and chapter, with the regnal year of the sovereign indicated before his name. Note that in legal citations an arabic numeral follows the name of a monarch in a succession of monarchs of the same name, instead of the capital roman numeral of more general usage (see par. 2:43).

[22]Companies Act, 1948, 19 & 20 George 5, ch. 38.

6:135   *Government reports, debates, and hearings.* These are cited as illustrated below. Citations of *hearings* must always indicate the committee and be identified as House or Senate (n. 26):

[23]H.R. Rep. No. 871, 78th Cong., 1st sess. 49 (1943).

[24]Federal Trade Comm'n, Report on Utility Corporations, S. Doc. No. 92, 70th Cong., 1st sess., pt. 71A (1935).

²⁵100 Cong. Rec. 8820 (1954) (remarks of
Senator Blank). [This is a citation to the bound
edition of the <u>Congressional Record</u>. The daily
edition, which is differently paginated, must be
indicated by day, month, and year.]

²⁶Hearings before the House Banking Committee
on the Housing Act of 1949, 81st Cong., 1st sess.,
ser. 9, pt. 4 at 109 (1949).

6:136   *Books and periodicals.* Authors are cited by surname alone,
unless works are mentioned by more than one author with
the same surname. Volume numbers, indicated in arabic
numerals, precede the author's name in a book citation
(n. 27); they precede the title of a periodical (n. 31). Page
numbers, not preceded by "p." ("pp."), follow book and
periodical titles, without punctuation between them. Facts
of publication consist of year date alone, except that the
edition of a book is noted if it is other than the first (n. 27).
For a work that is part of a series (numbered or unnum-
bered), issued by another than the author, the name of the
series and the number, if any, are noted in parentheses
before the publication date (n. 28). If the title of a work
incorporates the name of the author—whether of a person
or of an institution—the reference should be rearranged to
cite the author first. If the author is a government official,
this fact should be indicated by placing "U.S.," "N.Y.,"
or "Boston," as appropriate, before the name (n. 30).
The title of an article in a periodical or of an essay in the
collected works of an author is enclosed in quotation marks
(nn. 31, 32). In the latter case, notation of the volume number precedes the author's name (n. 32).

²⁷2 Holdsworth, A History of English Law
278 (6th ed. 1938).

²⁸Young, The Contracting Out of Work 145
(Research Ser. No. 1, Queen's University Industrial
Centre, 1964).

²⁹Black, Law Dictionary 85 (4th ed. 1951).
[This work is entitled <u>Black's Law Dictionary</u>.]

³⁰U.S., Comptroller of the Currency, Annual
Report, 1935 (1936). [The title of the work is
<u>Annual Report of the Comptroller of the Currency,
1935.</u>]

³¹Hutcheson, "A Case for Three Judges,"
48 Harv. L. Rev. 795 (1934).

³²4 Bentham, "Panopticon," Works 122–24 (1893).

6:137 *Loose-leaf services.* These services, which compile such information as statistical texts, regulations and rulings, editorial comment, recent cases, and citations to other pertinent authorities, frequently require citation. Reference is to the name of the service, omitting the publisher's name unless the omission would cause confusion. If the service is revised annually, the year date must be included. Paragraphs rather than pages are given:

³³2 P–H 1966 Fed. Tax Serv. par. 10182.

SECOND OR LATER REFERENCES

6:138 When a work has once been cited in complete form, later references to it are made in shortened forms. For these shortened titles or, where appropriate, the Latin abbreviation "ibid.," should be used. The use of "op. cit." and "loc. cit.," formerly common in scholarly references, is no longer recommended.

"IBID."

6:139 When references to the same work follow each other without any intervening reference, even though the references are separated by several pages, the abbreviation "ibid." (for the Latin *ibidem,* "in the same place") is used to repeat as much of the preceding reference as is appropriate for the new entry:

¹Max Plowman, An Introduction to the Study
of Blake (London: Gollancz, 1952), p. 32. [A first,
and therefore complete, reference to the work.]

²Ibid.
[With no intervening reference, a second mention
of the same page of Plowman's work requires only
"ibid." Notice that "ibid." is not underlined.]

³Ibid., p. 68.
[With no intervening reference since the last to

```
Plowman's work, "ibid." is still correct, but here
the reference is to a different page.]
```

6:140   Since "ibid." means "in the same *place*," it must not be used to repeat an author's name when references to two works by the same author follow each other without an intervening reference. Although repetition of the author's name in the second reference is the style preferred by many scholars, "idem" may be used. This Latin word, meaning "the same," is commonly used only in place of a person's name.[5] It may be abbreviated to "id." if the abbreviation is consistently used. Do not confuse "ibid." and "idem": note that in footnote 2 "ibid." stands for *all* the items of the preceding reference except page number. "Idem," referring only to a person, should not be used here:

```
1Arthur Waley, The Analects of Confucius
(London: George Allen & Unwin, 1938), p. 33.

2Ibid., p. 38.
```

6:141   On the other hand, in the following examples, "ibid." in the second footnote is incorrect, since it is used to repeat only the author's name from the preceding footnote, all the other items being changed. "Idem," meaning the same person, is correct here.

```
1Arthur Waley, The Analects of Confucius
(London: George Allen & Unwin, 1938), p. 33.

Wrong:
    2Ibid., Chinese Poems (London: George Allen
& Unwin, 1946), p. 51.

1Arthur Waley, The Analects of Confucius
(London: George Allen & Unwin, 1938), p. 33.

Right:
    2Idem, Chinese Poems (London: George Allen
and Unwin, 1946), p. 51.

[Repetition of the author's name would be equally
correct; but, again, consistency is necessary.
```

[5]References following legal style, however, employ "idem" (abbreviated as "id.") where this *Manual* stipulates "ibid."; legal style reserves "ibid." for references where there is no change in page or other part from the preceding reference.

Note that "idem" is a complete word, not an abbreviation, and is therefore not followed by a period.]

6:142   If a number of pages separate references to a given work, the writer may prefer for the sake of clarity to repeat the title—in shortened form, when desired—rather than to use "ibid." even though no reference to another work has intervened.

SHORTENED REFERENCES

6:143   Reference to a work that already has been cited in full form, *but not in the reference immediately preceding,* is made in one of two styles, which shall be called method A and method B.

6:144   *Method A.* Method A uses the author's last name (but not the first name or initials unless another author of the same surname has been cited), the title—in shortened form, if desired—and the specific reference.

6:145   *For a book,* a second or later reference to a work already cited in full form, but not in the reference immediately preceding, *omits* the facts of publication, series title, if any, edition (unless more than one edition of the same work has been cited), and total number of volumes. Thus pared down, the reference consists of author's last name, title of the work, with page, and volume number as well, if necessary. Note the full reference in footnote 1 and a later reference to the work as shown in (arbitrarily numbered) footnote 9:

[1]Gabriel Marcel, The Mystery of Being, 2 vols. (Chicago: Henry Regnery Co., 1960), 1:42.

[9]Marcel, Mystery of Being, 2:98–99.

Now consider another multivolume work, which has an overall title and different titles for the individual volumes, only one of which is referred to in the notes:

[3]Albert C. Baugh, ed., A Literary History of England, vol. 2: The Renaissance (1500–1660), by Tucker Brooke (New York: Appleton-Century-Crofts, 1948), p. 104.

A later reference to Brooke's work should carry only the title of his single volume, not the title of the *multivolume work* or the volume number referring to it:

> [9]Brooke, <u>Renaissance</u>, p. 130.

6:146   *For an article* in a magazine or journal, or for any component part of a work, such as a chapter in a book; or an essay, poem, or the like, in an anthology, a second or later reference to a work previously cited in its full form omits the name of the periodical, or book, or anthology, and omits also the volume number and date. The reference, then, consists of author's last name; title of the article, chapter, poem, essay—in shortened form, if desired—and page number. Examples of a full footnote reference to an article in a scholarly journal and its corresponding shortened form are shown in footnotes 4 and 7 below.

6:147   The following succession of footnotes illustrates the use of method A:

> [1]Max Plowman, <u>An Introduction to the Study of Blake</u> (London: Gollancz, 1952), pp. 58–59.
>
> [2]Plowman, note in William Blake's <u>The Marriage of Heaven and Hell</u>, reproduced in facsimile from an original drawing (London: J. M. Dent & Sons, 1927), pp. ix–xii. [Reference to another work by Plowman. The page numbers in small roman numerals are correct, since they are the style of numeral used in that part of the book containing Plowman's note.]
>
> [3]Review of <u>An Introduction to the Study of Blake</u>, by Max Plowman, <u>Times Literary Supplement</u>, 8 June 1952, p. 12. [Reference to a popular magazine, which is identified by date alone. See par. 6:78.]
>
> [4]Elspeth Longacre, "Blake's Conception of the Devil," <u>Studies in English</u> 90 (June 1937):384. [This reference is to a scholarly journal, which is cited by both volume number and date. See par. 6:74.]
>
> [5]Ibid. [The same as the reference immediately preceding.]

[6]Plowman, Blake, p. 125. [Reference to the first-noted work of Plowman, using the shortened title.]

[7]Longacre, "Blake's Devil," p. 381. [Another reference to Miss Longacre's journal article, using the shortened title. Other works having intervened since the complete reference in n. 4, "ibid." cannot be used.]

6:148 *Method B.* Method B uses the author's last name (without first name or initials unless another author of the same surname has been cited) and the page number (volume as well as page, if necessary). And this is all, unless more than one work by the same author has been cited previously, in which case the appropriate title—in shortened form, if desired—must be included in the reference. Works in which an association or institution or company stands as author must always include the title.

6:149 An example of a succession of footnotes illustrating the use of method B follows. It consists of the same works that are used to illustrate footnote practice under method A, thus pointing up the differences in the two methods:

[1]Max Plowman, An Introduction to the Study of Blake (London: Gollancz, 1952), pp. 58–59.

[2]Idem, note in William Blake's The Marriage of Heaven and Hell, reproduced in facsimile from an original drawing (London: J. M. Dent & Sons, 1927), pp. ix–xii. [Reference to another work by Plowman. Here "idem" is used to repeat the author's name. With no intervening reference, this is permissible (see par. 6:141). Note the small roman numerals used for page numbers, necessary in this case because the book itself so numbers its preliminary pages.]

[3]Review of An Introduction to the Study of Blake, by Max Plowman, Times Literary Supplement, 8 June 1952, p. 12. [Reference to a popular weekly periodical identified by date alone.]

[4]Elspeth Longacre, "Blake's Conception of the Devil," Studies in English 90 (June 1937): 384–88. [Reference to a scholarly journal identified by both volume and date.]

⁵Ibid. [The same as the reference immediately preceding.]

⁶Plowman, <u>Blake</u>, p. 125. [Since two works by Plowman have already been introduced, the title, here given in shortened form, is necessary.]

⁷Longacre, p. 381. [Another reference to Miss Longacre's article. Since only one work by her has been previously mentioned, the name and page number are sufficient under method B.]

SHORTENED TITLES

6:150   Generally speaking, titles of from two to five words need not be shortened, but length of the words may be considered and such a title as the following may be shortened as indicated:

<u>Perspectives in American Catholicism</u>   shortened to: <u>American Catholicism</u>·

6:151   A shortened title uses the key words of the main title, omitting an initial "A," "An," or "The." Titles beginning with such words as "A Dictionary of," "Readings in," "An Index to," would normally omit those words, using the topic as the short title:

<u>A Guide to Rehabilitation of   <u>Handicapped</u>
    the Handicapped</u>

<u>Bibliography of North American   <u>Folklore and</u>
    Folklore and Folksong</u>   <u>Folksong</u>

There are, however, dictionaries and bibliographies that cover a variety of topics: *An Index to General Literature, Biographical, Historical, and Literary Essays and Sketches, Reports and Publications of Boards and Societies Dealing with Education.* It would not do to include but one category in a short title; the only reasonable one is simply *Index.*

6:152   Following are examples of full titles with suitable corresponding shortened titles:

FULL MAIN TITLE   SHORT TITLE

<u>The Rise of the Evangelical   <u>Ministry in America</u>
    Conception of the Ministry
    in America</u>

Classification and Identifi- cation of Handwriting		Handwriting
The American Dream of Destiny and Democracy	Or:	American Dream Destiny and Democracy
Creation Legends of the Ancient Near East		Creation Legends
"Blake's Conception of the Devil"		"Blake's Devil"

Neither the order of the words of the original title nor the form of the words should be changed. *Creation Legends of the Ancient Near East,* for example, should not be given the short title *Near Eastern Legends.*

6:153   Normally, no part of a subtitle should be included in a shortened title. For such works as the following, the short titles come ready made: *The Pound Sterling: A History of English Money. Henry P. Davison: Biography.*

6:154   When a shortened title that might cause confusion is to be used, it is a convenience for the reader if the first full citation of the work notes that title (see par. 6:95).

CONTENT FOOTNOTES

6:155   Content (or substantive) footnotes consist of explanations or amplifications of the textual discussion and therefore resemble the text more than reference footnotes. When it is desirable to give the source of material included in a content footnote, the reference may be placed in one of several ways. It may be worked into a sentence, much as sources are sometimes worked into the text (see nn. 1, 2), or it may follow as a separate item (n. 3). In either case, whether the title is cited in full and whether the facts of publication are given depend upon whether the source has been referred to in a previous note:

[1]Detailed evidence of the great increase in the array of goods and services bought as income increases is shown in S. J. Prais and H. S. Houthaker, The Analysis of Family Budgets (Cambridge: Cambridge University Press, 1955), table 5, p. 52.

²Ernst Cassirer takes important notice of this in Language and Myth (pp. 59–62), and offers a searching analysis of man's regard for things on which his power of inspirited action may crucially depend. [Since the work has already been cited in full form, page reference only is required.]

³In 1962 the premium income received by all voluntary health insurance organizations in the United States was $9.3 billion, while the benefits paid out were $7.1 billion. Health Insurance Institute, Source Book of Health Insurance Data (New York: The Institute, 1963), pp. 36, 46.

⁴Professor D. T. Suzuki brings this out with great clarity in his discussion of "stopping" and "no-mindedness"; see, e.g., his chapter entitled "Swordsmanship" in Zen Buddhism and Its Influence on Japanese Culture (Kyoto: Eastern Buddhist Society, 1938).

CROSS-REFERENCES

6:156 Occasionally a writer finds it necessary to refer to material in another part of his paper. Such references often consist simply of page or note numbers, or both, inserted in parentheses in the text. Cross-references may also appear in footnotes. The words "above" (earlier in the paper) and "below" (later in the paper) are frequently used with page or other cross-references because they make it clear that the reference is to the paper in hand, not to another source mentioned. ("Supra" and "infra" are sometimes used, chiefly in law references, in place of "above" and "below.")

6:157 The word "see" is often used with cross-references; "cf." should be used only in the sense of "compare" and is not an alternate for "see."

¹For a detailed discussion of this matter see pp. 31–35 below.

6:158 A cross-reference such as "See n. 3 above" intended simply to refer to the title of a source is not permissible; a shortened title, or "ibid.," should be used instead (see pars. 6:138–54).

7 Bibliographies

7:1   The rules for bibliographical style in this chapter and the examples of bibliographical entries in chapter 8 apply mainly to papers in literature, history, and other nonscientific fields. The style for lists of references accompanying scientific papers is explained in chapter 12. For typing bibliographies, see par. 13:37.

HEADING

7:2   The bibliography lists the sources used in writing the paper—not necessarily every work examined but those that were found relevant. The quoting of pertinent passages from works dealing primarily with subjects different from the subject of the paper does not alone warrant the inclusion of those works in the bibliography.

7:3   Since a bibliography rarely includes all that has been written upon a given topic, a more accurate heading for this section of the paper would be, for example, "Selected Bibliography," "Works Cited," or "Sources Consulted." The last is especially suitable if the list includes such sources as personal interviews, lectures, tape recordings, radio or television broadcasts, which for the sake of convenience are by common usage included in a bibliography.

CLASSIFICATION

7:4   Unless the bibliography is very short, it is usually classified, divided into sections. Among the more common schemes is that of division according to the types of source materials used; another is that of works by an author and works about him; another, that of periods of time. There are many possible bases of classification, and the topic of the paper, its order of presentation, and its thesis will usually suggest the particular arrangement to be followed.

7:5   Sometimes the variety of source materials calls for further subdivision of the main classes, under second-level subheadings. Both levels of headings may be numbered or lettered.

7:6   Within the divisions and subdivisions, the entries should be arranged in a definite order. Although alphabetical order by surname of author is the most common, for some papers another order—for example, chronological, by date of publication—is more helpful. If a scheme other than alphabetical is used, it should be explained in a note either at the beginning of the bibliography or in a footnote on the first page of the bibliography.

BIBLIOGRAPHICAL ENTRIES COMPARED WITH FOOTNOTES

7:7   A bibliographical entry is similar to a full footnote reference in that it includes much the same material arranged in much the same order. Differences between the two in the way of presenting this material stem from the differences in purpose and placement. The purpose of the bibliographical entry is to list the work in full bibliographical detail: name(s) of author(s), full title of work, place, publisher, and date of publication. The purpose of the footnote, on the other hand, is primarily to inform the reader of the particular spot—page, section, or other—from which the writer of the paper has taken certain material in his text. The secondary purpose of the footnote—to enable the reader to find the source for himself—dictates the inclusion of the full bibliographical details in the first reference to a work (see par. 6:13). The differences in style of presentation between footnotes and bibliography are described below (pars. 7:8–10) and illustrated by the parallel examples in chapter 8.

7:8   In a footnote, the author's full name is given in the natural order, first name first, because there is no reason to reverse the order; in the bibliographical entry, the surname is given first because bibliographies are usually arranged in alphabetical order by surnames of authors.

7:9   Where there are two or more authors' names, each is reversed in the bibliography, for consistency and because the surnames are more important (see examples in pars. 8:4–6). (An alternate style, used by some writers but not recommended here, is to reverse only the first name—in order to alphabetize the item—and to give the following names in normal order.)

7:10   Whereas commas and parentheses are used in a footnote, periods are used in a bibliographical entry at the end of each main part—author's name, title of work, and facts of publication. Note, however, that references to periodicals usually retain the parentheses around the month and year when they follow the volume number (see examples in chap. 8).

7:11   Page numbers are listed in bibliographical entries only when the item is part of a whole work—a chapter in a book or an article in a periodical. When given, page numbers must be inclusive—first and last page of the relevant section (see pars. 6:82–83).

7:12   If the institution or department for which the paper is written requires a notation of the total number of pages for each book and pamphlet, the information is noted at the end of the entry—"Pp. xiv+450."

ALPHABETIZING AUTHORS' NAMES

7:13   Family names containing particles vary widely both in capitalization and in form of alphabetization when arranged with surname first as in bibliographies and indexes. The preference of the bearer of the name—or tradition concerning it—as reflected in *Webster's Biographical Dictionary,* should be followed in alphabetizing family names with particles. Note the wide variations in the following list:

```
à Beckett, Gilbert Abbott      Gogh, Vincent van
Becket, Thomas à               Hindenburg, Paul von
Broek, Jacobus ten             La Fontaine, Jean de
de Gaulle, Charles             Ramée, Marie Louise de la
De La Rey, Jacobus             Vandervelde, Emile
de Vere, Aubrey Thomas         Velde, Jan van de
De Vries, Hugo                 Von Schrenk, Hermann
```

7:14   Names beginning with "Mc," "M'," or "Mac" should be alphabetized as though they all began with "Mac":

```
McAdam, John Loudon            M'Carthy, Justin
Macarthur, Mary Reid           MacCracken, Henry Noble
Macaulay, Rose                 McCutcheon, John T.
McCarthy, Charles              Macdonald, Flora
```

7:15   Names beginning with "St." or "Ste" should be alphabetized as though they began with "Saint" or "Sainte." The name of a saint, however, should be alphabetized according to the personal name:

```
Augustine, Saint               Saint-Simon, Henri
Sainte-Beuve, Charles Augustin
```

7:16   Compound surnames are alphabetized by the first name in the compound:

```
Watts-Dunton, Theodore
Temple Lang, John
```

7:17   Germanic names spelled with an umlaut are alphabetized as though "ä" were "ae," "ö" were "oe," and "ü" were "ue."

7:18   Spanish names which consist of given name (or names) and paternal name and maternal name joined with the conjunction *y* are alphabetized under the paternal name. Many names omit the conjunction, however, and in such a name as Manuel Ramón Albeniz, one does not know whether the father's surname is Ramón or whether it is a second given name. If the facts cannot be determined, the library catalog may often serve as a guide.

7:19   A writer who has adopted a religious name sometimes writes under that name alone, preceded by the appropriate title. Sometimes he adds his surname to the religious name. Alphabetize by the name rather than the title:

```
Eva Catherine, Sister          Hayden, Cuthbert, Father
```

7:20   Chinese and Arabic names are the chief non-Western names to cause problems in alphabetizing. In Chinese the family name precedes the given name and so the name is not reversed in alphabetizing:

```
Lin Yutang                    Mao Tse-tung
```

In Arabic, names beginning with *Abd, abu-,* or *ibn* are usually alphabetized under these elements; those beginning with *al-* ("the") are alphabetized by the element following this particle:

```
Abd-al-Hakam                  ibn-Khaldun
Gazali, al-
```

7:21   Authors with the same surname and the same first initial, one identified by initials alone, one by a single given name, and one by the same name plus a middle name, are alphabetized as follows:

```
Adams, J. B.
Adams, John
Adams, John Quincy
```

7:22   When reversed, names with "Sr." or "Jr." or a roman numeral are punctuated as follows:

```
Brownell, Arthur P., Jr.
Edwards, Ira Raymond III
```

7:23   Works published under a pseudonym should be listed under the author's real name. The pseudonym may be enclosed in brackets and placed after the name if desired:

```
Baker, Ray Stannard [David Grayson]. Adventures
in Contentment.
```

7:24   In a succession of works by the same author, the name is given for the first entry, and an eight-space line (the underlining key struck eight times) ending with a period takes its place in subsequent entries. The entries are arranged alphabetically by title or chronologically by date.

```
Tillich, Paul. Love, Power, and Justice.
   New York: Oxford University Press, 1960.
_____. Systematic Theology. 3 vols.
   Chicago: University of Chicago Press, 1951-63.
```

7:25   Titles of works *edited* by the author or of works written by him in *collaboration* with others should not be alphabetized along with works written by him alone. In a list including all three categories, put the edited titles after the works written by the author in question, using an eight-space line for his name, followed by a comma and "ed."

7:26   The works of which he is a coauthor follow the edited works, but the author's name must be repeated here. Do *not* use an eight-space line for a coauthor's name, or to take the place of two or more coauthors.

7:27   A long bibliography of works by one man may carry a heading including his name, which would then not appear with each item. Works edited by him would either be under a subheading or begin with the abbreviation "Ed." Works he wrote in collaboration with others would begin, for example, "With Joseph P. Jones and John Q. Adams."

7:28   A work for which no author (editor, compiler, or other) is known appears in a bibliography under the title of the work, alphabetized by the first word, or the first word following an initial article.

TITLES OF WORKS

7:29   Capitalization of titles must agree with the scheme adopted for citing titles in footnotes and elsewhere in the paper (see pars. 4:5–12).

7:30   Underlining the titles of whole publications—books, periodicals, and all other works whose titles are underlined in footnotes and text—is optional in the bibliography, but the same style must be followed throughout the bibliography.

7:31   Quotation marks must be used around titles of articles and other component parts of whole publications (except in scientific papers; see chap. 12).

7:32   Foreign words and phrases in English titles must be underlined, except that titles entirely in a foreign language are not underlined if the option is taken of not underlining the titles of whole publications (see par. 7:30). A title in a foreign language that is enclosed in quotation marks is not underlined.

ANNOTATION

7:33   A bibliography may be annotated either in whole or in part. The annotation need not be a complete sentence grammatically, but it should begin with a capital and end with a period. The first line begins on the line following the entry proper and may be indented if desired:

Thompson, Oscar, ed. International Cyclopedia
    of Music and Musicians. New York: Dodd, Mead &
    Co., 1938.
        An admirable work which brings Grove up
    to date and deals adequately with contemporary
    music and American composers.

8 Sample Footnote References and Corresponding Bibliographical Entries

8:1   The following examples illustrate footnote and bibliographical forms exclusive of those used in citations of public documents (chap. 9) and in scientific fields (chap. 12).

8:2   The abbreviations "N." and "B." stand respectively for footnote entry and bibliographical entry.

BOOKS

8:3   *One author*

N.   [1]Paul Tillich, Systematic Theology, 3 vols. (Chicago: University of Chicago Press, 1951–63), 1:9.

B.   Tillich, Paul. Systematic Theology. 3 vols. Chicago: University of Chicago Press, 1951–63.

8:4   *Two authors*

N.   [2]Walter E. Houghton and G. Robert Stange, Victorian Poetry and Poetics (Cambridge: Harvard University Press, 1959), p. 27.

B.   Houghton, Walter E., and Stange, G. Robert. Victorian Poetry and Poetics. Cambridge: Harvard University Press, 1959.

8:5   *Three authors*

N.   [3]Bernard R. Berelson, Paul F. Lazarsfeld, and William McPhee, Voting (Chicago: University of Chicago Press, 1954), pp. 93–95.

B.   Berelson, Bernard R.; Lazarsfeld, Paul F.; and McPhee, William. Voting. Chicago: University of Chicago Press, 1954.

8:6   *More than three authors*

N.   [4]Jaroslav Pelikan et al., <u>Religion and the</u> <u>University</u>, York University Invitation Lecture Series (Toronto: University of Toronto Press, 1964), p. 109.

B.   Pelikan, Jaroslav; Ross, M. G.; Pollard, W. G.; Eisendrath, M. N.; Moeller, C.; and Wittenberg, A. <u>Religion and the University.</u> York University Invitation Lecture Series. Toronto: University of Toronto Press, 1964.

8:7   *No author given*

N.   [5]<u>The Lottery</u> (London: J. Watts, [1732]), pp. 20–25.

B.   <u>The Lottery</u>. London: J. Watts, [1732].

8:8   *No author given; name supplied*

N.   [6][Henry K. Blank], <u>Art for Its Own Sake</u> (Chicago: Nonpareil Press, 1910), p. 8.

B.   [Blank, Henry K.] <u>Art for Its Own Sake</u>. Chicago: Nonpareil Press, 1910.

8:9   *Pseudonymous author; real name supplied* (see pars. 6:20–22)

N.   [7]Elizabeth Cartright Penrose [Mrs. Markham], <u>A History of France</u> (London: John Murray, 1872), p. 9.

B.   Penrose, Elizabeth Cartright [Mrs. Markham]. <u>A History of France</u>. London: John Murray, 1872.

8:10   *Institution, association, or the like, as "author"*

N.   [8]Special Libraries Association, <u>Directory</u> <u>of Business and Financial Services</u> (New York: Special Libraries Association, 1963), p. 21.

B.   Special Libraries Association. <u>Directory of Business and Financial Services</u>. New York: Special Libraries Association, 1963.

8:11   *Editor as "author" (same form used for compiler)*

N.   [9]J. N. D. Anderson, ed., <u>The World's Religions</u> (London: Inter-Varsity Fellowship, 1950), p. 143.

B.   Anderson, J. N. D., ed. The World's Religions. London: Inter-Varsity Fellowship, 1950.

8:12 *Author's work translated by another (same form if edited by another)*

N.   [10]Ivar Lissner, The Living Past, trans. J. Maxwell Brownjohn (New York: G. P. Putnam's Sons, 1957), p. 58.

B.   Lissner, Ivar. The Living Past. Translated by J. Maxwell Brownjohn. New York: G. P. Putnam's Sons, 1957.

8:13 *Author's work contained in his collected works*

N.   [11]Samuel Taylor Coleridge, The Complete Works of Samuel Taylor Coleridge, ed. W. G. T. Shedd, vol. 1: Aids to Reflection (New York: Harper & Bros., 1884), p. 18.

B.   Coleridge, Samuel Taylor. The Complete Works of Samuel Taylor Coleridge. Edited by W. G. T. Shedd. Vol. 1: Aids to Reflection. New York: Harper & Bros., 1884.

8:14 *Separately titled volume in a multivolume work with a general title and editor*

N.   [12]Gordon N. Ray, gen. ed., An Introduction to Literature, 4 vols. (Boston: Houghton Mifflin Co., 1959), vol. 2: The Nature of Drama, by Hubert Hefner, pp. 47–49.

B.   Ray, Gordon N., gen. ed. An Introduction to Literature. 4 vols. Boston: Houghton Mifflin Co., 1959. Vol. 2: The Nature of Drama, by Hubert Hefner.

8:15 *Separately titled volume in a multivolume work with a general title and one author*

N.   [13]Will Durant, The Story of Civilization, vol. 1: Our Oriental Heritage (New York: Simon & Schuster, 1942), p. 88.

B.   Durant, Will. The Story of Civilization. Vol. 1: Our Oriental Heritage. New York: Simon & Schuster, 1942.

8:16 *Book in a series*

N.   [14]Verner W. Clapp, The Future of the Research Library, Phineas W. Windsor Series in

Librarianship, no. 8 (Urbana: University of
Illinois Press, 1964), p. 92.

B.   Clapp, Verner W. <u>The Future of the Research
      Library</u>. Phineas W. Windsor Series in
      Librarianship, no. 8. Urbana: University
      of Illinois Press, 1964.

8:17   *Paperback series*

N.   [15]George F. Kennan, <u>American Diplomacy,
      1900–1950</u> (Chicago: University of Chicago Press,
      1951; Phoenix Books, 1970), p. 48.

B.   Kennan, George F. <u>American Diplomacy, 1900–1950</u>.
      Chicago: University of Chicago Press,
      1951; Phoenix Books, 1970.

8:18   *Edition other than the first*

N.   [16]William R. Shepherd, <u>Historical Atlas</u>,
      8th ed. (New York: Barnes & Noble, 1956), p. 62.

B.   Shepherd, William R. <u>Historical Atlas</u>. 8th ed.
      New York: Barnes & Noble, 1956.

If the edition were edited by someone other than the author,
the edition number would be followed by the words "Edited
by _____."

8:19   *Reprint edition*

For a work that has been reprinted, it is important to give
publisher and date of the reprint following the usual information about the book as originally issued:

N.   [17]Gunnar Myrdal, <u>Population: A Problem for
      Democracy</u> (Cambridge: Harvard University Press,
      1940; reprint ed., Gloucester, Mass.: Peter
      Smith, 1956), p. 9.

B.   Myrdal, Gunnar. <u>Population: A Problem for
      Democracy</u>. Cambridge: Harvard University
      Press, 1940; reprint ed., Gloucester,
      Mass.: Peter Smith, 1956.

8:20   *Title within a title*

A title of another work appearing within an underlined title
is enclosed in double quotation marks:

N.   [18]Arnold B. Come, <u>An Introduction to Barth's</u>
          <u>"Dogmatics" for Preachers</u> (Philadelphia:
          Westminster Press, 1963), pp. 90–92.

B.   Come, Arnold B. <u>An Introduction to Barth's</u>
          <u>"Dogmatics" for Preachers</u>. Philadelphia:
          Westminster Press, 1963.

8:21   When the title of a book occurs within a title that is in
           quotation marks, such as the title of an article in a journal,
           the book title is underlined:

N.   [19]Cedric H. Whitman, "Two Passages in the
          <u>Ion</u> of Euripides," <u>Classical Philology</u> 59
          (October 1964):257.

B.   Whitman, Cedric H. "Two Passages in the <u>Ion</u>
          of Euripides." <u>Classical Philology</u> 59
          (October 1964):257–59.

8:22   When the title of an article appears within the title of
           another article, single quotation marks are used:

"Comment on 'How to Make a Burden of the Public Debt'"

8:23   *Book with named author of introduction, preface, or*
           foreword

N.   [20]Dag Hammarskjöld, <u>Markings</u>, with a
          Foreword by W. H. Auden (New York: Alfred
          A. Knopf, 1964), p. 9.

B.   Hammarskjöld, Dag. <u>Markings</u>. Foreword by W. H.
          Auden. New York: Alfred A. Knopf, 1964.

If Auden's authorship of the foreword were more significant than Hammarskjöld's book here, the following would
be the correct form:

N.   [21]W. H. Auden, Foreword to <u>Markings</u>, by
          Dag Hammarskjöld (New York: Alfred A. Knopf,
          1964), p. ix.

B.   Auden, W. H. Foreword to <u>Markings</u>, by Dag
          Hammarskjöld. New York: Alfred A. Knopf,
          1964.

8:24   *Book in a foreign language with English title supplied*

N.   [22]Maria Turlejska, <u>Rok przed kleska</u> [The
          year before the defeat] (Warsaw: Wiedza
          Powszechna, 1962), p. 445.

B.   Turlejska, Maria. <u>Rok przed kleska</u> [The year
            before the defeat]. Warsaw: Wiedza
            Powszechna, 1962.

Note that the English translation of the title is neither
underlined nor enclosed in quotation marks.

8:25   *Component part by one author in a work edited by another*

N.   [23]Paul Tillich, "Being and Love," in
        <u>Moral Principles of Action</u>, ed. Ruth N. Anshen
        (New York: Harper & Bros., 1952), p. 663.

B.   Tillich, Paul. "Being and Love." In <u>Moral
            Principles of Action</u>, pp. 661–72. Edited
            by Ruth N. Anshen. New York: Harper &
            Bros., 1952.

8:26   *Book privately printed*

N.   [24]John G. Barrow, <u>A Bibliography of
        Bibliographies in Religion</u> (Austin, Tex.:
        By the Author, 716 Brown Bldg., 1955), p. 25.
        [Street address not always given.]

B.   Barrow, John G. <u>A Bibliography of Bibliographies
            in Religion</u>. Austin, Tex.: By the Author,
            716 Brown Bldg., 1955.

8:27   *Secondary source of quotation*

N.   [25]<u>Jesuit Relations and Allied Documents</u>,
        vol. 59, n. 41, quoted in [or "cited by"]
        Archer Butler Hulbert, <u>Portage Paths</u> (Cleveland:
        Arthur H. Clark, 1903), p. 181.

B.   <u>Jesuit Relations and Allied Documents</u>, vol. 59,
            n. 41. Quoted in [or "cited by"] Archer
            Butler Hulbert, <u>Portage Paths</u>, p. 181.
            Cleveland: Arthur H. Clark, 1903.

REPORTS—PUBLISHED

8:28   *Author named*

N.   [1]John H. Postley, <u>Report on a Study of
        Behavioral Factors in Information Systems</u>
        (Los Angeles: Hughes Dynamics, [1960]), p. 15.

B.   Postley, John H. <u>Report on a Study of Behavioral
            Factors in Information Systems</u>. Los
            Angeles: Hughes Dynamics, [1960].

8:29   *Chairman of committee named*

N.   ²Report of the Committee on Financial
Institutions to the President of the United
States, by Walter W. Heller, Chairman (Washington, D.C.: Government Printing Office, 1963),
p. 12.

B.   Report of the Committee on Financial Institutions
to the President of the United States.
By Walter W. Heller, Chairman. Washington,
D.C.: Government Printing Office, 1963.

8:30   For reports published in microform see par. 8:42.

PROCEEDINGS—PUBLISHED

8:31   N.   ¹Industrial Relations Research Association,
Proceedings of Third Annual Meeting (Madison,
Wis.: n.p., 1951), p. 30. [The date of the
meeting is often part of the title.]

B.   Industrial Relations Research Association.
Proceedings of Third Annual Meeting.
Madison, Wis.: n.p., 1951.

UNPUBLISHED REPORTS AND PROCEEDINGS

8:32   Titles of unpublished reports and proceedings are enclosed in quotation marks. When not given in the title,
place and date follow it. There may also be the notation
"Typewritten" or "Mimeographed" in parentheses (see
par. 8:45).

YEARBOOKS

8:33   *Department of government*

N.   ¹U.S., Department of Agriculture, Yearbook
of Agriculture, 1941 (Washington, D.C.:
Government Printing Office, 1941), p. 683.

B.   U.S. Department of Agriculture. Yearbook of
Agriculture, 1941. Washington, D.C.:
Government Printing Office, 1941.

8:34   *Article in a yearbook*

N.   ²G. M. Wilson, "A Survey of the Social
and Business Use of Arithmetic," Second Report

of the Committee on Minimal Essentials in
Elementary–School Subjects, in Sixteenth
Yearbook of the National Society for the Study
of Education, pt. 1 (Bloomington, Ill.: Public
School Publishing Co., 1917), pp. 20–22.

B.   Wilson, G. M. "A Survey of the Social and
Business Use of Arithmetic." Second Report
of the Committee on Minimal Essentials
in Elementary–School Subjects, in Sixteenth
Yearbook of the National Study of
Education, pt. 1. Bloomington, Ill.:
Public School Publishing Co., 1917.

ARTICLES IN JOURNALS OR MAGAZINES

8:35   *Article in a journal*

N.   [1]Don Swanson, "Dialogue with a Catalogue,"
Library Quarterly 34 (December 1963):115.

B.   Swanson, Don. "Dialogue with a Catalogue."
Library Quarterly 34 (December 1963):
113–25.

See paragraph 6:74. In citing journals that are numbered
only by issue, not volume, note the style set forth in paragraph 6:76; and journals that publish volumes in successive
series, numbered or lettered, paragraph 6:77.

8:36   *Article in a magazine*

N.   [2]Barbara W. Tuchman, "If Asia Were Clay
in the Hands of the West," Atlantic, September
1970, p. 72.

B.   Tuchman, Barbara W. "If Asia Were Clay in the
Hands of the West." Atlantic, September
1970, pp. 68–84.

(See also par. 6:78.)

ARTICLES IN ENCYCLOPEDIAS

8:37   *Signed article*

N.   [1]Encyclopaedia Britannica, 11th ed., s.v.
"Blake, William," by J. W. Comyns–Carr.

B.   Encyclopaedia Britannica, 11th ed. S.v. "Blake,
William," by J. W. Comyns–Carr.

8:38   *Unsigned article*

N.   [2]Encyclopedia Americana, 1963 ed., s.v.
        "Sitting Bull."

B.   Encyclopedia Americana, 1963 ed. S.v. "Sitting
            Bull."

(See also pars. 6:101, 8:39.)

NEWSPAPERS

8:39   N.   [1]San Francisco Chronicle, 5 June 1971.

Bibliographical entry is the same in this case, but see paragraph 8:40.

N.   [2]"Amazing Amazon Region," New York Times,
        12 January 1969, sec. 4, p. Ell.

B.   "Amazing Amazon Region." New York Times,
            12 January 1969, sec. 4, p. Ell.

Several matters to be considered in referring to newspapers are discussed in paragraphs 6:97–100.

8:40   In the bibliographical entries shown for journal, magazine, encyclopedia, and newspaper articles, the style assumes in each case only one reference to the publication. If the writer has used the issues of a periodical covering a considerable period of time, this fact may be indicated by giving the title of the periodical with the dates as in notes 1 or 2, as may be appropriate:

[1]Saturday Review, 2, 16, 30 July; 2, 20, 27
August 1966.

[2]Times (London), 4 January–6 June 1964.

Two or more articles in an encyclopedia or similar reference work may be contained in one bibliographical entry:

Columbia Encyclopedia, 3d ed. (1963). S.v.
            "Custer, George Armstrong," "Sioux
            Indians."

Several articles in the same magazine or professional journal should always be listed separately, each under its author.

140

BOOK REVIEWS

8:41   N.   [1]Benjamin DeMott, review of Briefing for
a Descent into Hell, by Doris Lessing, in
Saturday Review, 13 March 1971, p. 25.

   B.   DeMott, Benjamin. Review of Briefing for a
            Descent into Hell, by Doris Lessing.
            Saturday Review, 13 March 1971, pp. 25–26.

MICROFORM REPRODUCTIONS

8:42   N.   [1]Godwin C. Chu and Wilbur Schramm.
Learning from Television: What the Research Says
(Bethesda, Md.: ERIC Document Reproduction
Service, ED 014 900, 1967), p. 3.

   B.   Chu, Godwin C., and Schramm, Wilbur. Learning
            from Television: What the Research Says.
            Bethesda, Md.: ERIC Document Reproduction
            Service, ED 014 900, 1967.

(See also par. 6:118.)

UNPUBLISHED MATERIALS

MANUSCRIPT COLLECTIONS

8:43   An individual document in a manuscript collection, like
a page in a book, may be referred to in a footnote but
seldom appears in a bibliography. If mentioned, it should
be the last item in the bibliographical entry, rather than
the first as in the footnote:

   N.   [1]Gen. Joseph C. Castner, "Report to the
War Department," 17 January 1927, Modern
Military Records Division, Record Group 94,
National Archives, Washington, D.C.

   B.   Washington, D.C. National Archives. Modern
            Military Records Division. Record Group
            94. Gen. Joseph C. Castner, "Report to
            the War Department," 17 January 1927.

   N.   [2]Stimson Diary and War Letters, February
1918, Henry L. Stimson Papers, Yale University,
New Haven, Conn.

   B.   New Haven, Conn. Yale University. Henry L.
            Stimson Papers.

N.   ³London, British Museum, Arundel MSS,
   285, fol. 165b.

B.   London. British Museum. Arundel MSS.

8:44   Note that the title of a document is enclosed in quotation
marks, but that such general designations as *diary*, *letter*,
memorandum are capitalized but neither quoted nor underlined in footnote and bibliographical entries. (See also
par. 6:119.)

THESES AND OTHER PAPERS

8:45   Note that "unpublished" is not included in the designation,
the title within quotation marks indicating that the work is
not published:

N.   ¹O. C. Phillips, Jr., "The Influence of
   Ovid on Lucan's Bellum civile" (Ph.D. dissertation, University of Chicago, 1962), p. 14.

B.   Phillips, O. C., Jr. "The Influence of Ovid on
        Lucan's Bellum civile." Ph.D. dissertation,
        University of Chicago, 1962.

N.   ²American Institute of Planners, Chicago
   Chapter, "Regional Shopping Centers Planning
   Symposium," Chicago, 1942. (Mimeographed.)

B.   American Institute of Planners, Chicago Chapter.
        "Regional Shopping Centers Planning
        Symposium." Chicago, 1942. (Mimeographed.)

N.   ³H. P. Luhn, "Keyword-in-Context Index
   for Technical Literature," paper presented at
   the 136th meeting of the American Chemical
   Society, Atlantic City, N.J., 14 September 1959.

B.   Luhn, H. P. "Keyword-in-Context Index for
        Technical Literature." Paper presented
        at the 136th meeting of the American
        Chemical Society, Atlantic City, N.J.,
        14 September 1959.

N.   ⁴Morristown (Kansas) Children's Home,
   Minutes of Meetings of the Board of Managers,
   1945-55, meeting of 6 May 1950. (Typewritten.)

B.   Morristown (Kansas) Children's Home. Minutes
        of Meetings of the Board of Managers,
        1945-55. (Typewritten.)

MULTIPLE REFERENCES CONTAINED
IN A SINGLE FOOTNOTE

8:46   The individual references in a footnote citing several works are separated with semicolons:

N.   [1]See Samuel P. Langley, James Smithson (Washington, D.C.: Smithsonian Institution, 1904), pp. 18, 19; Paul Oehser, Sons of Science (New York: Henry Schuman, 1949), pp. 1, 9–11; and Webster True, The First Hundred Years of the Smithsonian Institution: 1846–1946 (Washington, D.C.: Smithsonian Institution, 1946), p. 2.

The bibliographical entries would be alphabetized separately:

B.   Langley, Samuel P. James Smithson. Washington, D.C.: Smithsonian Institution, 1904.

B.   Oehser, Paul. Sons of Science. New York: Henry Schuman, 1949.

B.   True, Webster. The First Hundred Years of the Smithsonian Institution: 1846–1946. Washington, D.C.: Smithsonian Institution, 1946.

INTERVIEWS

8:47   Since interviews may be of considerable value as sources, they may be included in a bibliography, even though they are not written material.

N.   [1]Interview with John Nought, Primus Realty Company, San Jose, California, 12 May 1962.

B.   Nought, John. Primus Realty Company, San Jose, California. Interview, 12 May 1962.

9 Public Documents

9:1   The form used for citing public documents should be one that makes them readily accessible to anyone wishing to locate them in a library. The arrangement of information on the title pages of the documents themselves, its amount, and its complexity raise puzzling questions of how much of the information it is necessary to include and in what order it should be set down in the footnote. Here reference to the card catalog of the library can be of great help, although it is not a safe guide in such matters as capitalization and punctuation of titles, which for public documents as well as for other references must follow the scheme of the paper. When in doubt of how much to include in a reference, it is better to err on the side of giving too much rather than too little information.

9:2   The name of the country, state, city, town, or other government district (e.g., U.S., Great Britain, Illinois, Baltimore) is given first in the citation of an official publication issued by one of them or under its auspices. Then comes the name of the legislative body, court, executive department, bureau, board, commission, or committee. The name of the office rather than the title of the officer should be given except where the title of the officer is the only name of the office, as, for example, "Illinois, State Entomologist." The name of the division, regional office, etc., if any, follows the name of the department, bureau, or commission. Thus the "author" of a document might read: U.S., Department of Labor, Manpower Administration, Office of Manpower Policy, Evaluation, and Research. Following the name of the author, the title of the document, if any, should be given. From this point, the information noted is dependent largely upon the nature of the material.

9:3   Generally speaking, references to public documents do not include the facts of publication. When, however, the document has a personal author whose name is included (as it should be) in the reference, it is best to show the facts of publication. For some such references the date of publication may be the only clue to the date of the work (see par. 9:7, n. 5).

UNITED STATES GOVERNMENT DOCUMENTS

9:4   The United States government publishes its official documents in two main categories—those originating in the Congress and those originating in the executive departments.

CONGRESSIONAL DOCUMENTS

9:5   The proceedings of each house of Congress, together with the presidential messages to it, are published in the *Journal,* separately for House and Senate, at the close of each session. The debates appear in the *Congressional Record* (since 1873). Besides the bills and resolutions initiated by the Congress, there are the materials furnished to it by committees, governmental agencies, and executive officers of government—reports, hearings, miscellaneous documents. Citations to all of them must include, in addition to the authorizing body, the number, session, and date of the Congress; title and number (if any) of the document; and, in some instances, the title of the work in which the document can be found, with relevant volume and page number(s).

9:6   The letters "N." and "B." stand, respectively, for footnote entry and bibliographical entry.

9:7   *Bills, reports, and miscellaneous documents*

N.   [1]U.S., Congress, House, A Bill to Require Passenger-Carrying Motor Vehicles Purchased for Use by the Federal Government to Meet Certain

Safety Standards, H.R. 1341, 86th Cong., 1st
sess., 1959, pp. 1–4.

B.   U.S. Congress. House. A Bill to Require
        Passenger-Carrying Motor Vehicles
        Purchased for Use by the Federal Government
        to Meet Certain Safety Standards. H.R.
        1341, 86th Cong., 1st sess., 1959.

N.   [2]U.S., Congress, Senate, Planning in
        Metropolitan Areas, S. Rept. 821 to Accompany
        S. 855, 88th Cong., 2d sess., 1963, pp. 3–5.

B.   U.S. Congress. Senate. Planning in Metropolitan
        Areas, S. Rept. 821 to Accompany S. 855,
        88th Cong., 2d sess., 1963.

N.   [3]U.S., Congress, Senate, Report of the
        Federal Trade Commission, S. Doc. 92, 70th
        Cong., 1st sess., 1935, pt. 71A.

B.   U.S. Congress. Senate. Report of the Federal
        Trade Commission. S. Doc. 92, 70th
        Cong., 1st sess., 1935.

N.   [4]U.S., Congress, Senate, Committee on
        Foreign Relations, Technical Assistance and
        Related Programs. S. Rept. 1956, 84th Cong.,
        2d sess., 1960, Senate Miscellaneous Reports
        on Public Bills 3: 184–85.

B.   U.S. Congress. Senate. Committee on Foreign
        Relations. Technical Assistance and
        Related Programs. S. Rept. 1956, 84th
        Cong., 2d sess., 1960. Senate Miscellaneous
        Reports on Public Bills, vol. 3.

N.   [5]U.S., Congress, Joint Economic Committee,
        The Low-Income Population and Economic Growth,
        by Robert J. Lampman, Joint Committee Print,
        Study Paper 12 (Washington, D.C.: Government
        Printing Office, 1959), pp. 14–15.

B.   U.S. Congress. Joint Economic Committee.
        The Low-Income Population and Economic
        Growth, by Robert J. Lampman. Joint
        Committee Print, Study Paper 12. Washing-
        ton, D.C.: Government Printing Office,
        1959.

N.   [6]U.S., Congress, House, The Drug Abuse
        Control Amendments of 1965, 89th Cong., 1st
        sess., 1965, Journal, 10 March 1965, pp. 337–42.

B.   U.S. Congress. House. The Drug Abuse Control
      Amendments of 1965. 89th Cong., 1st
      sess., 1965. Journal, 10 March 1965.

9:8   Hearings should be cited by title. If the "author" does
      not indicate the committee before whom the hearings were
      held, the committee should be named in the reference.

N.   [7]U.S., Congress, House, Committee on Ways
      and Means, Narcotics, Marihuana, and Barbi-
      turates, Hearings before a subcommittee of the
      House Committee on Ways and Means on H.R. 3490.
      82d Cong., 1st sess., 1951, p. 4.

B.   U.S. Congress. House. Committee on Ways and
      Means. Narcotics, Marihuana, and Barbi-
      turates. Hearings before a subcommittee of
      the House Committee on Ways and Means on
      H.R. 3490, 82d Cong., 1st sess., 1951.

9:9   Congressional bills and resolutions are published in pam-
      phlet form. When a bill is enacted into law, it becomes a
      part of the *Statutes at Large*. In the interim between its
      having been introduced into one of the houses and its
      passage and publication as a law in the *Statutes*, a bill is
      cited to the slip bill, or to the *Congressional Record* if
      it is contained therein:

N.   [8]U.S., Congress, House, An Act to Amend
      the Bank Holding Company Act of 1956, Pub. L.
      89-485, 89th Cong., 2d sess., 1966, H.R. 7371,
      p. 3.

B.   U.S. Congress. House. An Act to Amend the Bank
      Holding Company Act of 1956. Pub. L.
      89-485, 89th Cong., 2d sess., 1966,
      H.R. 7371.

9:10 Congressional debates are printed in the *Congressional
      Record*. Unless the subject of the speech, or merely of
      the remarks, is mentioned in the text, it is proper to include
      it in the citation:

N.   [9]U.S., Congress, Senate, Senator Blank
      speaking for the Amendment of the Standing Rules
      of the Senate, S. Res. 103, 89th Cong., 1st
      sess., 14 November 1965, Congressional Record
      102:6522. [A reference to the bound volume,

which is differently paged from the Daily
Digest.]

B.   U.S. Congress. Senate. Senator Blank speaking
for the Amendment of the Standing Rules
of the Senate. S. Res. 103, 89th Cong.,
1st sess., 14 November 1965. Congressional
Record, vol. 102.

9:11   Presidential proclamations, executive orders, and any
other documents submitted by the president, or orders to
be published, are carried in the *Federal Register*, which
is issued on every day following a government working
day:

N.   [10]U.S., President, Proclamation, "Supplemental Quota on Imports of Long—Staple Cotton,"
Federal Register 15, no. 196, 10 October 1950,
6801—2.

B.   U.S. President. Proclamation. "Supplemental
Quota on Imports of Long—Staple Cotton."
Federal Register 15, no. 196, 10 October
1950, 6801—2.

9:12   The public papers of the presidents of the United States
are collected in two large works:

N.   [11]J. D. Richardson, ed., Compilation of
the Messages and Papers of the Presidents, 1789—
1897, 53d Cong., 2d sess., 1907, House Miscellaneous Document No. 210, pts. 1—10, 10 vols.
(Washington, D.C.: Government Printing Office,
1907), 4:16.

B.   Richardson, J. D., ed. Compilation of the
Messages and Papers of the Presidents,
1789—1897, 53d Cong., 2d sess., 1907,
House Miscellaneous Document No. 210,
pts. 1—10. 10 vols. Washington, D.C.:
Government Printing Office, 1907.

N.   [12]U.S., President, Public Papers of the
Presidents of the United States (Washington,
D.C.: Office of the Federal Register, National
Archives and Records Service, 1953—   ), Dwight
D. Eisenhower, 1956, pp. 222—23.

B.   U.S. President. Public Papers of the Presidents
of the United States. Washington, D.C.:
Office of the Federal Register, National

Archives and Records Service, 1953–
Dwight D. Eisenhower, 1956.

9:13   After their passage, bills and joint and concurrent resolutions are cited as statutes. Those that have gone into effect during the year are published in the *Statutes at Large* (n. 13 below), which since 1939 have been issued annually at the close of the calendar year. Later, the statutes are published in the *United States Code. Code* citation is preferred when it is available (n. 14). As a matter of convenience to the reader, a statute is sometimes given a parallel citation to the *Statutes at Large* (n. 15):

N.   [13]Administrative Procedure Act, Statutes at Large 60, sec. 10, 243 (1946).

B.   Administrative Procedure Act. Statutes at Large, vol. 60 (1946).

N.   [14]Declaratory Judgment Act, U.S. Code, vol. 28, secs. 2201–2 (1952). [Citations to the Code are always to section number, not page.]

B.   Declaratory Judgment Act. U.S. Code, vol. 28 (1952).

N.   [15]Labor Management Relations Act (Taft-Hartley Act), Statutes at Large 61, sec. 301(a), 156 (1947), U.S. Code, vol. 39, sec. 185(a) (1952).

B.   Labor Management Relations Act (Taft-Hartley Act). Statutes at Large, vol. 61 (1947). U.S. Code, vol. 39 (1952).

9:14   The United States Constitution is referred to by article and section (by clause as well, if relevant). If the reference is to an amendment, that must be cited by number following *Constitution*:

N.   [16]U.S., Constitution, art. I, sec. 4.

B.   U.S. Constitution. Art. I, sec. 4.

N.   [17]U.S., Constitution, amend. XIV, sec. 2.

B.   U.S. Constitution. Amend. XIV, sec. 2.

9:15   The several government commissions, such as the Federal Communications Commission, Federal Trade Commission,

Securities and Exchange Commission, also publish bulletins, circulars, reports, study papers, and the like. Often, those communications are classified as House or Senate Documents:

N.   [18]U.S., Congress, Senate, Report of the Federal Trade Commission on Utility Corporations, S. Doc. 92, 70th Cong., 1st sess., 1935, pt. 71A.

B.   U.S. Congress. Senate. Report of the Federal Trade Commission on Utility Corporations. S. Doc.. 92, 70th Cong., 1st sess., 1935.

EXECUTIVE DEPARTMENT DOCUMENTS

9:16   Executive department documents consist of reports of executive departments and bureaus, bulletins, circulars, and miscellaneous materials. Many departmental publications are classified in series, and some have personal authors whose names are given in the citations (n. 2 below). It is not desirable, however, to cite government publications by names of personal authors. Few libraries catalog them except under the name of the sponsoring government agency. (J. D. Richardson, editor of the *Compilation of the Messages and Papers of the Presidents*, is a notable exception.)

N.   [1]U.S., Department of Health, Education, and Welfare, Proceedings, 1961 Conference of the Surgeon-General, Public Health Service, and Chief, Children's Bureau, with State and Territorial Health Officers, 8-10 August 1961, pp. 8-10.

B.   U.S. Department of Health, Education, and Welfare. Proceedings, 1961 Conference of the Surgeon-General, Public Health Service, and Chief, Children's Bureau, with State and Territorial Health Officers, 8-10 August 1961.

N.   [2]U.S., Department of Agriculture, Farm Security Administration and Bureau of Agricultural Economics Co-operating, Analysis of 70,000 Rural Rehabilitation Farmlands, by E. L. Kirkpatrick, Social Research Report No. 9 (Washington, D.C.: Government Printing Office, 1938), pp. 19-32.

B.   U.S. Department of Agriculture. Farm Security
      Administration and Bureau of Agricultural
      Economics Co–operating. Analysis of 70,000
      Rural Rehabilitation Farmlands, by E. L.
      Kirkpatrick. Social Research Report No. 9.
      Washington, D.C.: Government Printing
      Office, 1938.

N.   [3]U.S., Department of State, Declaration
      of the U.N. Conference on Food and Agriculture,
      War Documents Series Pubn. No. 2162 (1944),
      pp. 6–8.

B.   U.S. Department of State. Declaration of the
      U.N. Conference on Food and Agriculture.
      War Documents Series Pubn. No. 2162 (1944).

N.   [4]U.S., Department of State, Public Roads
      Program in the Philippines, Treaties and Other
      International Acts Series 1584, Pubn. 2805
      (1947), p. 3. [The number 1584 is the number
      of the "treaty" as assigned by the State
      Department.]

B.   U.S. Department of State. Public Roads Program
      in the Philippines. Treaties and Other
      International Acts Series 1584, Pubn.
      2805 (1947).

N.   [5]U.S., Department of Interior, Office of
      Indian Affairs, Annual Report of the Commissioner
      of Indian Affairs to the Secretary of the
      Interior, for the Fiscal Year Ended 30 June
      1932, p. 24.

B.   U.S. Department of Interior. Office of Indian
      Affairs. Annual Report of the Commissioner
      of Indian Affairs to the Secretary of the
      Department of the Interior, for the Fiscal
      Year Ended 30 June 1932.

N.   [6]U.S., Department of Commerce, Bureau of
      the Census, Fifteenth Census of the United
      States, 1930: Population, 2:98.

B.   U.S. Department of Commerce. Bureau of the
      Census. Fifteenth Census of the United
      States, 1930: Population, vol. 2.

N.   [7]U.S., Department of Commerce, Bureau of
      the Census, United States Census of Population:
      1960, vol. 1, Characteristics of the Population,
      pt. 6, California.

B.   U.S. Department of Commerce. Bureau of the
      Census. United States Census of Population:
      1960. Vol. 1, Characteristics of the
      Population, pt. 6, California.

9:17   Since 1950, treaties have been published in the *United
States Treaties and Other International Agreements* (n. 8),
the annual bound volumes of the papers as they were numbered and published by the Department of State in pamphlet
form in the series Treaties and Other International Acts
(par. 9:16, n. 4). With the inauguration of the new series,
publication was discontinued in the *Statutes at Large*.
Multilateral treaties appear in the Treaty Series of the
United Nations (n. 10), although usually a year or more
after their signature. Treaties predating 1950 may be found
(depending upon their nature and date) in the Treaty Series
of the League of Nations, the Treaty Series and Executive
Agreement Series of the Department of State, and in the
Statutes at Large (n. 9):

N.   [8]U.S., Department of State, United States
      Treaties and Other International Agreements,
      vol. 14, pt. 2, "Nuclear Weapons Test Ban,"
      TIAS No. 5433, 5 August 1963.

B.   U.S. Department of State. United States Treaties
            and Other International Agreements, vol.
            14, pt. 2. "Nuclear Weapons Test Ban,"
            TIAS No. 5433, 5 August 1963.

N.   [9]U.S., Statutes at Large, vol. 43, pt. 2
      (December 1923--March 1925), "Naval Armament
      Limitation Treaty," 26 February 1922.

B.   U.S. Statutes at Large, vol. 43, pt. 2 (Decem-
            ber 1923--March 1925). "Naval Armament
            Limitation Treaty," 26 February 1922.

N.   [10]United Nations, Treaty Series, Treaties
      and International Agreements Registered or Filed
      and Reported with the Secretariat of the United
      Nations, vol. 250 (1956), No. 3516, "Denmark
      and Italy: Convention concerning Military
      Service," 15 July 1954, p. 45.

B.   United Nations. Treaty Series. Treaties and
            International Agreements Registered or
            Filed and Reported with the Secretariat

of the United Nations, vol. 250 (1956),
No. 3516, "Denmark and Italy: Convention
concerning Military Service," 15 July 1954.

STATE AND LOCAL GOVERNMENT DOCUMENTS

9:18 Citations to state and local government documents are in essentially the same form as those to United States government documents:

N. [1]Illinois, Constitution (1848), art. 5, sec. 2. [Ordinarily, the date of a constitution is indicated only when it is not in force.]

B. Illinois. Constitution (1848).

N. [2]Kentucky, Revised Statutes, Annotated (Baldwin, 1943). [The style used in referring to an annotated revision made by William E. Baldwin in 1943.]

B. Kentucky. Revised Statutes, Annotated (Baldwin, 1943).

N. [3]Ohio, Judicial Organization Act, Statutes (1830) 3:1671-78.

B. Ohio. Judicial Organization Act. Statutes (1830), vol. 3.

N. [4]New York, N.Y., "Good Samaritan" Law, Administrative Code (1965), sec. 67-3.2.

B. New York, N.Y. "Good Samaritan" Law. Administrative Code (1965).

BRITISH GOVERNMENT DOCUMENTS

9:19 Citations to British government documents, like their counterparts in United States documents, should begin with the name of the authorizing body under which they were issued—Parliament, Public Record Office, Foreign Office, Ministry of Transport, and so on, always preceded by "Great Britain."

9:20 English statutes are always cited by name, regnal year of the sovereign, and chapter number. Names of sovereigns are abbreviated and arabic numerals are used throughout the references. Before publication in the *Statutes* or in the *Public General Acts and Church Assembly Measures*, statutes are cited as in note 1; when they are published in one or the other compilation, their citations follow the forms of notes 2 and 3:

N.   ¹Great Britain, Laws, Statutes, etc.,
       Coroner's Act, 1954, 2 & 3 Eliz. 2, ch. 31.

B.   Great Britain. Laws, Statutes, etc. Coroner's
            Act, 1954. 2 & 3 Eliz. 2, ch. 31.

N.   ²Great Britain, Laws, Statutes, etc.,
       Transport Act, 1962, 10 & 11 Eliz. 2, ch. 46,
       Halsbury's Statutes of England (2d ed.),
       42: 565–68 (pt. 1, sec. 3–6).

B.   Great Britain. Laws, Statutes, etc. Transport
            Act, 1962. 10 & 11 Eliz. 2, ch. 46.
            Halsbury's Statutes of England (2d ed.),
            vol. 42.

N.   ³Great Britain, Laws, Statutes, etc.,
       Trustee Savings Banks Act, 1964, 12 Eliz. 2,
       ch. 4, Public General Acts and Church Assembly
       Measures, 1964, pt. 1, p. 6 (sec. 2/3).

B.   Great Britain. Laws, Statutes, etc. Trustee
            Savings Banks Act, 1964. 12 Eliz. 2, ch. 4.
            Public General Acts and Church Assembly
            Measures, 1964, pt. 1.

9:21   The *Parliamentary Papers* are bound annually in consecutive volumes of *Bills*, *Reports*, and *Accounts and Papers*. Each of these has its own series of volume numbers, which means that any one title is, for example, volume 2 in its own series and volume 10 of the *Parliamentary Papers* for the year. In the volumes of *Reports*, the separate, individually paged documents are arranged alphabetically by their subjects. The three series are composed of "command" papers[1] and are cited as such (n. 1 below), with number and title, if desired:

N.   ¹Great Britain, Parliament, Parliamentary
       Papers (Commons), 1962–63, vol. 19 (Reports,

[1]For the numbering and abbreviations for consecutive series of command papers, see the University of Chicago *Manual of Style*, 12th edition, p. 393.

vol. 8), Cmnd. 2062, December 1962, "Report
of the Ministry of Health for the Year Ended
31 December 1962," ch. 2, pp. 8–10 [of the
report].

B.   Great Britain. Parliament. Parliamentary Papers
(Commons), 1962–63,. vol. 19 (Reports,
vol. 8). Cmnd. 2062, "Report of the
Ministry of Health for the Year Ended
31 December 1962."

9:22   The *Sessional Papers* (not to be confused with the *Parliamentary Papers,* which also are sometimes referred to as *Sessional Papers*) have been published since 1938–39 following each session of Parliament separately for the two houses. The series is divided into eight titles — five for the House of Commons and three for the House of Lords. The annual series of *Papers* is identified by year date alone, but each of the eight titles has its individual set of volume numbers. A citation to these *Sessional Papers* can be deceiving, since some of the volumes are made up of separate papers that are individually paged and arranged either chronologically by day or alphabetically by subject. Citations should be made, not to page numbers, but to the specific document by its title, with pertinent numbered sections or paragraphs if the paper is long. The books have well-arranged tables of contents and indexes, and locating a particular paper is no problem. (See nn. 1 and 2, below.)

N.   [1]Great Britain, Parliament, Sessional
Papers (Commons), 1962–63, Votes and Proceedings,
19 March 1963, "Navy Supplementary Estimate,
1962–63" (Supply). [No volume number in this
case, since there was but one in 1962–63. The
arrangement is alphabetical by subject,
"Supply."]

B.   Great Britain. Parliament. Sessional Papers
(Commons), 1962–63. Votes and Proceedings,
19 March 1963, "Navy Supplementary Estimate, 1962–63" (Supply).

N.   [2]Great Britain, Parliament, Sessional
Papers (Lords), 1962–63, Public Bills, vol. 1,
"Contracts of Employment," sec. 2.

B.   Great Britain. Parliament. Sessional Papers
(Lords), 1962–63. Public Bills, vol. 1,
"Contracts of Employment."

9:23   Since 1909 the *Parliamentary Debates* have been published separately for the two houses. The name *Hansard* (for the original printer of the *Debates*) is properly omitted from the title of volumes issued since 1891, but it still has official sanction and is sometimes used even now (n. 2). Both series and volume numbers are necessary:

N.   [1]Great Britain, Parliament, Parliamentary Debates (Commons), 5th series, 721 (1965): 779-87.

B.   Great Britain. Parliament. Parliamentary Debates (Commons), 5th series, vol. 721 (1965).

N.   [2]Great Britain, Parliament, Hansard's Parliamentary Debates (Lords), 5th series, 58 (1924):11-15.

B.   Great Britain. Parliament. Hansard's Parliamentary Debates (Lords), 5th series, vol. 58 (1924).

9:24   The *British Foreign and State Papers* are arranged within the volumes alphabetically by country and, further, by subject:

N.   [1]Great Britain, Foreign Office, British Foreign and State Papers, 1852-53, "Austria: Proclamation of the Emperor Annulling the Constitution of 4th March, 1849," 41:1298-99.

B.   Great Britain. Foreign Office. British Foreign and State Papers, 1852-53, "Austria: Proclamation of the Emperor Annulling the Constitution of 4th March, 1849," vol. 41.

9:25   Reports are issued in pamphlet form by the several ministries, commissions, committees, and the like:

N.   [1]Great Britain, Office of the Minister of Science, Committee on Management and Control of Research, Report, 1961, p. 58.

B.   Great Britain. Office of the Minister of Science, Committee on Management and Control of Research. Report, 1961.

9:26   The early records entitled *Calendar of . . .* are arranged chronologically. In some, numbered items—grants, leases, warrants, pardons, and so on—appear within a "calendar" of no uniform duration (n. 1). Dates are essential, therefore, in identifying the items:

N.   [1]Great Britain, Public Record Office,
        Calendar of the Patent Rolls, Eliz. [1], vol. 4
        (1566–69): Calendar 66 (17 November 1566––16
        November 1567), 2 May 1567, no. 455, Pardon for
        Richard Byngham, pp. 63–64.

B.   Great Britain. Public Record Office. Calendar
        of the Patent Rolls, Eliz. [1], vol. 4
        (1566–69), Calendar 66: 2 May 1567,
        no. 455.

N.   [2]Great Britain, Public Record Office,
        Calendar of State Papers, Domestic, of the Reign
        of Charles 2, vol. 209 (1667): 12 July 1667,
        Earl of Carlisle to Williamson, p. 289.

B.   Great Britain. Public Record Office. Calendar
        of State Papers, Domestic, of the Reign
        of Charles 2, vol. 209 (1667): 12 July
        1667, Earl of Carlisle to Williamson.

N.   [3]Great Britain, Public Record Office,
        Calendar of Treasury Books, vol. 32 (1718),
        pt. 2: 27 February, "Royal Warrant to the Clerk
        of the Signet. . . ."

B.   Great Britain. Public Record Office. Calendar
        of Treasury Books, vol. 32 (1718), pt. 2:
        27 February, "Royal Warrant to the Clerk
        of the Signet. . . ."

N.   [4]Great Britain, Public Record Office,
        List and Analysis of State Papers, Foreign
        Series, Eliz. [1] (1 August 1589––30 June 1590),
        vol. 1: III, Spain, no. 637, "Spanish Agents
        in England."

B.   Great Britain. Public Record Office. List and
        Analysis of State Papers, Foreign Series,
        Eliz. [1] (1 August 1589––30 June 1590),
        vol. 1: III, Spain, no. 637.

LEAGUE OF NATIONS AND UNITED NATIONS DOCUMENTS

9:27   For these documents, the authorizing body, the topic of
        the paper, the document number, and the date must be given
        in the references:

N.   [1]League of Nations, Secretariat, <u>Appli-</u>
       <u>cation of Part II of the Opium Convention</u>
       (O.C. 114) (1923), p. 5.

B.   League of Nations. Secretariat. <u>Application of</u>
            <u>Part II of the Opium Convention</u> (O.C. 114)
            (1923).

N.   [2]United Nations, Economic and Social
       Council, Social Commission, 17th Session,
       <u>Reappropriation of the Role of the Social</u>
       <u>Commission: Report of the Secretary-General</u>
       (E/CN. 5/400), 16 February 1966, pp. 9–10.

B.   United Nations. Economic and Social Council,
            Social Commission, 17th Session. <u>Reappro-</u>
            <u>priation of the Role of the Social</u>
            <u>Commission: Report of the Secretary-General</u>
            (E/CN. 5/400), 16 February 1966.

N.   [3]United Nations, General Assembly, 17th
       Session, 8 October 1966, <u>Report of the Special</u>
       <u>Committee on the Situation with Regard to the</u>
       <u>Implementation of the Declaration on the Granting</u>
       <u>of Independence to Colonial Countries and</u>
       <u>Peoples</u> (A/5238), annex 1, p. 3.

B.   United Nations. General Assembly, 17th Session,
            8 October 1966. <u>Report of the Special</u>
            <u>Committee on the Situation with Regard to</u>
            <u>the Implementation of the Declaration on</u>
            <u>the Granting of Independence to Colonial</u>
            <u>Countries and Peoples</u> (A/5238).

N.   [4]United Nations, World Health Organiza-
       tion, <u>Toxic Hazards of Pesticides to Man:</u>
       <u>Twelfth Report of the Expert Committee on</u>
       <u>Insecticides</u> (WHO Technical Report Series,
       no. 227), 1962, pp. 6–10.

B.   United Nations. World Health Organization.
            <u>Toxic Hazards of Pesticides to Man:</u>
            <u>Twelfth Report of the Expert Committee</u>
            <u>on Insecticides.</u> WHO Technical Report
            Series, no. 227, 1962.

10 Tables

10:1   If tables are to serve satisfactorily the purpose for which they are made, they not only must be accurately compiled but must be so arranged that they can be easily read and interpreted. To these ends careful spacing, ruling, arrangement of headings, and, finally, the placing of the tables with respect to the text all contribute.

NUMBERING

10:2   In general every table should be given a number and a title, even though there may be few tables in the paper. (A very simple tabulation introduced in such a way that a caption seems unnecessary should not be given a number.) The order in which the tables are mentioned in the text determines the numbering.

10:3   Tables in an appendix should be numbered consecutively with the tables in the text. That is, if the last table in the text is table 52, the first table in the appendix is table 53.

POSITION

10:4   Numbering tables aids the typist in placing them. All text references to a table should be by number—for example, "As table 3 shows . . ." or "(see table 3)"—never by an introductory phrase such as "in the following table:" With all references by number and no colon demanding immediate inclusion of the table, the text may be typed to the end of the page or the paragraph and the table inserted where its size permits.

10:5   Ideally, each table should be placed as close to the first reference to it as possible. If space permits, however, it

159

is best to finish the paragraph of text in which the reference occurs before inserting the table. If a table cannot be accommodated in the remaining space available for it on a given page, it should be placed on the next page, either (if it is long enough) by itself or else with text following it. If a table is just a few lines too long for a page, it may be shortened by using one-and-one-half-line spacing instead of double spacing.

10:6   In typing tables with text, three spaces should be left above and three spaces below each table (i.e., the table number is typed on the third space following the text, and the text is continued on the third space below the bottom rule).

SIZE

10:7   Most tables may be typed so that columns run the long way of the page. A table may occupy the full width of the typed page or, if the number and width of columns permit, less than the full width. In either case each table must be centered horizontally upon the page (see table 1).

LONG AND NARROW

10:8   When a table is long and narrow, space may be saved by doubling up — dividing it in equal parts and placing them side by side (see table 2). Note the vertical double line separating the two parts.

WIDE

10:9   If a table is too wide for the page, it should be turned lengthwise — that is, the paper is put in the typewriter sideways and the table is typed so that the columns run the short way of the paper. Table number and title are at the binding side of the page. A table so typed is called a *broadside* table (see table 6). No text should be typed on a page containing a broadside table.

10:10   If too wide to be accommodated broadside, a table may be arranged on two facing pages (see table 7). This is done physically by turning the first page over so that the typed side is on the back and thus faces the next page (the other side of the first page, now the front, remains blank).[1] The parts of the table must be of the same dimensions on both pages, and special care in typing will be required to insure that the appropriate figure in each column is exactly in line with the item in the stub (i.e., first column) to which it belongs.

10:11   Tables too wide to be accommodated on the 8½-by-11-inch page in either of the ways described may be typed on two or more pages, which then may be pasted together and reduced to page size by a suitable photographic process; or, less satisfactorily for the use of any paper that is to be bound and placed in a library, a large table may be folded. (See pars. 11:29–31.)

CONTINUING LONG

10:12   Long tables may be continued from page to page. The table number and the caption are typed at the beginning of the table; the table number only on succeeding pages, written, for example, "TABLE 2 – *Continued*." Ordinarily, the boxheadings above the columns are repeated on every page, except that in a continued broadside table in which the pages face each other, the headings need not be repeated on the second page (and the fourth, sixth, etc.). In a table that is continued, the bottom rule is omitted except on the last page, at the end of the table.

CAPTIONS

10:13   It is necessary to give each numbered table a title, or caption. If a very brief tabulation is introduced in such a way that a caption seems unnecessary, the tabulation should not be given a table number.

10:14   In typing the table number and caption, center "TABLE 00" all in capital letters on a line by itself, with the number in arabic numerals. Center the caption, also in capital letters, on the second space below the table number. If the

---

[1]If the paper is to be bound, a note to the binder, in addition to the correct placement of the pages, will insure accurate results.

caption is longer than the width of the table, set it in two or more lines, arranged in inverted pyramid form and single spaced. If table captions contain chemical, physical, or mathematical expressions conventionally expressed in small letters, rather than capitals, these expressions should be so typed, even though the rest of the caption is in capitals (see also par. 10:15).

10:15   If the captions of most of the tables are two or more lines in length, time and space would be saved by using a different style of caption from that just described. Type the table number as just directed, but place it at the edge of the table rather than in the center; add a period and a dash and continue with the caption, typing the first and all succeeding full lines the full width of the table and centering the last, shorter line. Capitalization may either follow the rules for capitalizing titles of works (par. 4:6) or the system where only the first word and all proper nouns and proper adjectives are capitalized:

```
TABLE 21.--Probable rate of damage per foot-
candle for thirty light sources expressed in
       percentage relative to zenith day
```

Type all captions in a consistent style throughout the paper.

BOXHEADINGS

10:16   Column headings, called boxheadings, may be of one level or of two or more levels. The first level, spanner headings, are set off by rules and centered above the subsumed headings below (see table 5). Center each heading above the column it identifies, leaving the same amount of blank space above and below the headings. Never place a horizontal rule immediately beneath a heading lest the rule be mistaken for underlining of the words. To allow for the vertical rules, leave at least one space at either end of the longest line of each heading.

10:17   Boxheadings may be typed vertically if necessary to save space. They should be set so as to read up from the bottom of the page (see table 6). Where runover lines are unavoidable in a boxheading, they should be typed single space.

10:18   It is a convenience for the columns to be numbered when the textual discussion refers to individual columns. The numbers should be enclosed in parentheses and centered on the first line below the boxheadings. The stub column is not numbered. (See table 3.)

CUT-IN HEADINGS

10:19   To avoid an excessive number of levels of boxheadings (three at the outside), it is sometimes possible to insert a head that cuts across the body of the table and applies to the tabular matter lying below it (see table 5). Cut-in heads should be centered and capitalized in the same style as the boxheadings.

CAPITALIZATION

10:20   Adapt the capitalization of the boxheadings to that of the caption according to the following scheme: If the caption either is in capitals throughout or is capitalized as a title of a work (see par. 4:6), the boxheadings should be capitalized as titles. But if the caption employs capitals only for first word, proper nouns, and proper adjectives (see par. 10:15), the capitalization of the boxheadings should agree.

STUB

10:21   The left-hand column of a table, known as the stub, has no boxheading unless one is necessary for identification. Only the first word and proper names are capitalized. If the individual items require runover lines, they are indented to the third space. When an item is subdivided, however, the subdivisions are indented three spaces and any runovers are indented further:

```
Coastal district vs. interior
   district . . . . . . . . .
```

```
But:
Relative to issue
       price:
    1923–27 . . . .
    1949–55 . . . .
```

Another way to show subdivision in a stub is to underline the main entry but not the subdivisions, aligning all at the left (table 4).

10:22   If a *Total*, *Mean*, or *Average* appears in the stub, the word should be indented. If both *Total* and *Grand total* are given, the latter is indented further (see par. 10:40).

10:23   If the open space between the end of a line in the stub and the columnar matter to which it refers is such that the eye does not move easily from one to the other, period leaders (spaced periods) should connect the two (see table 4). If one table in a paper requires leaders, all should have them.

OMISSIONS

10:24   In a long column of figures, zero preceding a decimal point may be omitted from all entries except the first and the last. Degree and dollar signs (°, $) must appear at the top of each column where relevant and after every break in a column, such as rules above totals and cut-in headings.

10:25   If all the figures in a table are in thousands or millions, space may be saved by omitting the relevant zeroes and noting the fact at the end of the caption, as, for example, "(Figures in millions)." (See table 4.)

10:26   A blank space in a column should be indicated by spaced period leaders, which should be at least three in number and centered with respect to the longest number in the column (see table 7) or the number necessary to occupy the full width of the column. Use one of these styles consistently.

ALIGNMENT

10:27   The items in the stub should be aligned with their related items in the columns. If the stub item occupies more than

one line and the column entry one, align on the last line of
the stub; if both contain more than one line, align on the
first line and omit leaders:

```
Mean water content
    (percent) . . . . . . 69.6

But:
C₂(35"-50"+) (fresh      Dark grayish brown
    till, slightly        (10 YR 4/2) boul-
    oxidized)             dery loamy sand;
                          massive structure;
                          pH of 6.42
```

10:28   Vertically, in a column of figures align all decimal points
and commas. Note that every figure of 1,000 or more must
have a comma (see par. 2:51). Align also dollar signs and
plus, minus, plus-minus, and equals signs. When the number of digits varies, allow for the longest number.

ABBREVIATIONS AND SYMBOLS

10:29   Although prohibited for the most part in text, abbreviations
and symbols are legitimate space-savers in box- and cut-in
headings and in the main body of tables, but not in captions
(except mathematical and chemical symbols). Standard
abbreviations should be used if they exist; if they do not,
the writer may devise his own, explaining them in a note
or key unless they are self-explanatory. Abbreviations
must be consistent for all tables.

10:30   Symbols that cannot be made with the typewriter should
be inserted by hand, using permanent black ink (india ink
preferred). A plus sign made with the hyphen and diagonal
line (∕) is not acceptable, but the sign made with the
hyphen on the typewriter and the vertical bar inserted by
hand in black ink is satisfactory.

FOOTNOTES TO TABLES

10:31   Footnotes to tables may be of three kinds: source notes,
general notes, and notes referring to specific parts of the
table. The term "source note" is self-explanatory: if a
writer has not compiled the data for a table himself, he

must identify his source. General notes might include re-marks on the reliability of the data presented or of the way they were collected or handled; such notes apply to the entire table. These two kinds of notes do not require refer-ence symbols in the table; they are introduced, respectively, by the words SOURCE(S) and NOTE(S).

10:32 Notes to specific parts of a table require reference sym-bols. If the table consists of information in words only, superior numerals may be used as reference indexes. If the table consists wholly or partly of figures, either su-perior letters (^{a,b}) or symbols ($*, **$) should be used. If it includes mathematical or chemical formulas requiring notes, symbols rather than superior letters or figures must be employed.

10:33 Footnotes to tables must not be numbered in the same series as text notes. A new series of reference numbers, or symbols, is begun for each table.

10:34 The notes should appear in the following order: source notes, general notes, and notes to specific parts; and they should be placed immediately below the table, not at the foot of the page below lines of text. Begin the first note on the second space below the bottom rule of the table. Each note should have a paragraph indention and the notes should be typed to the full width of the table, except under double-page tables. Single-space runover lines, but double-space between notes.

10:35 If a table employing symbols as reference marks requires no more than three, double and triple asterisks may be used, but if more than three are required, additional sym-bols must be used: † (dagger), ‡ (double dagger), # (number sign). The use of more than three asterisks or of a combi-nation of asterisks and superior letters is not permissible. The same scheme of reference marks should be used for all tables.

RULING

10:36 Since some institutions specify that all tables be ruled and others allow considerable latitude, it is advisable for the

TABLE 1

MULTIPLE CORRELATION COEFFICIENTS
OF PROBABILITY FUNCTIONS

Range of Values	No. Observed Values
0–.199	15
.2–.399	1
.4–.599	1

TABLE 2

CASES FILED, TERMINATED, AND PENDING IN THE COURT OF APPEALS
FOR THE THIRD CIRCUIT, FISCAL YEARS 1940–1949, INCLUSIVE

Fiscal Year	Commenced	Terminated	Pending	Fiscal Year	Commenced	Terminated	Pending
1940	322	360	170	1945	299	268	226
1941	285	350	102	1946	197	274	149
1942	292	222	172	1947	266	216	199
1943	353	302	223	1948	287	250	236
1944	276	304	195	1949 (1st half)	128	113	251

TABLE 3

OLDER WORKERS IN FRANCE BY OCCUPATION, 1956

Occupation	Men		Women	
	Aged 65 and Over (in Thousands) (1)	Percentage Following Principal Occupation (2)	Aged 65 and Over (in Thousands) (3)	Percentage Following Principal Occupation (4)
Farmowners	508	42	652	14
Farm laborers	140	20	124	3
Owners of business and industry .	302	40	352	26
Professional workers and managers of business and industry . . .	202	21	82	7
Clerical workers	148	12	122	3
Manual workers	482	18	376	13
Artists, clergy, army, police . .	70	17	4	50
Domestic service	50	32	366	16
Never employed	18	. . . . .	948	. . . . .
Total	1,920	28	3,026	10

167

TABLE 4

ESTIMATED NATIONAL INCOME OF INDIA, AT 1948-49 PRICES
1900-1901 TO 1950-51, BY SELECTED YEARS
(Money Amounts in Millions of Rupees)

	1900-1901	1910-11	1920-21	1930-31	1940-41	1950-51
Total income						
Amount	51,090	62,410	64,690	76,840	86,460	91,920
Index	100.0	122.1	126.6	150.4	169.2	179.9
Agricultural production						
Amount	39,760	44,330	38,070	45,980	45,340	44,050
Index	100.0	111.5	95.7	115.6	114.0	110.8
All other industries						
Amount	11,330	18,080	26,620	30,860	41,120	48,070
Index	100.0	159.6	234.9	272.4	362.9	424.8

SOURCE: V. K. R. V. Rao, A. K. Ghosh, M. V. Divatia, and Um Datta, eds.,
Papers on National Income and Allied Topics, Indian Conference on Research in
National Income 2 (Bombay: Asia Publishing House, 1962):22-23, table 3.

TABLE 5

EFFECT OF A SINGLE 24-HOUR EXPOSURE TO 33 DEGREES C. DURING
DIFFERENT PERIODS OF PUPAL DEVELOPMENT,
REMAINDER OF TIME AT 25 DEGREES C.

Period at 33 Degrees	No. Flies Emerged	Time in Days			Percentage of Development					
		Low Temp.	High Temp.	Total	Per day		Low Temp.	High Temp.	Total	Total −100
					Low Temp.	High Temp.				
Males										
First day	61	3.31	1.00	4.31±0.009	23.47	27.54	77.68	27.54	105.22	+5.22
Second day	64	3.27	1.00	4.27±0.009	23.47	27.54	76.74	27.54	104.28	+4.28
Third day	62	3.14	1.00	4.14±0.020	23.47	27.54	73.69	27.54	101.23	+1.23
Fourth day	66	3.00	0.92	3.92+0.005	23.47	27.54	70.41	25.33	95.74	−4.26
Females										
First day	39	3.08	1.00	4.08±0.009	24.87	28.57	76.59	28.57	105.16	+5.16
Second day	53	2.94	1.00	3.94±0.006	24.87	28.57	73.11	28.57	101.68	+1.68
Third day	58	2.82	1.00	3.82±0.011	24.87	28.57	70.13	28.57	98.70	−1.30
Fourth day	51	3.00	0.86	3.66±0.007	24.87	28.57	74.64	24.57	99.21	−0.79

168

TABLE 6

VALUE ADDED BY MANUFACTURER PER PRODUCTION WORKER (IN DOLLARS), SOUTH BEND STANDARD METROPOLITAN AREA AND SEVEN SELECTED STANDARD METROPOLITAN AREAS, 1947

Census Groups and Code Number	South Bend	South Bend Rank among Selected Standard Metropolitan Areas	Chicago	Indianapolis	St. Louis	Detroit	Toledo	Grand Rapids	Milwaukee
20. Food & kindred products .	9,183	5	9,340	8,585	8,777	8,296	7,600	7,709	11,932
23. Apparel & related products .	3,797	11	5,397	5,017	4,588	5,170	4,495	5,081	4,732
24. Lumber & products, except furniture	5,629	2	5,503	3,700	4,464	7,569	5,124	5,168	5,262
26. Paper & allied products . .	7,111	6	6,605	7,286	5,781	6,491	6,629	7,858	7,804
27. Printing & publishing industries	9,767	4	9,125	10,040	8,660	11,528	10,350	8,990	7,888
32. Stone, clay & glass products	4,033	11	6,558	6,058	5,663	6,563	10,284	6,049	6,383
33. Primary metal industries . .	6,397	4	6,689	4,321	5,599	5,600	6,668	5,263	6,453
34. Fabricated metal products .	5,351	10	6,534	5,037	5,687	6,569	5,759	5,884	6,928
35. Machinery, except electrical	6,048	10	6,656	5,502	5,756	6,847	7,298	7,022	6,368
36. Electrical machinery	6,613	6	6,682	6,614	6,054	6,862	5,823	. . . [a]	6,243
39. Miscellaneous manufactures .	4,755	7	6,042	5,521	4,760	5,825	4,608	5,239	4,642

SOURCE: U.S. Department of Commerce, Bureau of the Census, Census of Manufactures: 1947, vol. 3, Statistics by States (Washington, D.C.: Government Printing Office, 1948), pp. 205–9, 308–18, 343–50, 479–81, 483, 648–49.

[a] Complete figures are not provided by the Census.

169

TABLE 7

CASE LOAD PER JUDGESHIP FOR THE NORTHERN DISTRICT OF FLORIDA
FOR THE FISCAL YEARS 1940–48, INCLUSIVE
(CASES FILED PER JUDGE)

Fiscal Year	Number of Judges, Florida (Northern)	Total Civil Cases per Judge		Criminal Cases per Judge	
		Florida (Northern)	84 Districts	Florida (Northern)	84 Districts
1940	1	95	153	191	178
1941	1	104	164	247	165
1942	1	103	168	147	174
1943	1	79	158	105	190
1944	1	70	169	161	211
1945	1	98	295	239	209
1946	1	131	321	125	171
1947	1	106	271	110	173
1948	1	85	205	206	167

NOTE: During the entire period covered by the table, there were three judges assigned to the southern district of Florida and one to the northern district. In all these years except the fiscal year 1948, there was one "roving judge" for both districts, but as almost all his time was spent in the southern district, the case load for 1940–48 has been figured on the basis of one judge in the northern district.

Because case-load figures are given to the nearest whole number, it is not always possible to derive exact totals by adding the component parts.

student to check into the matter with the appropriate staff member. The following suggestions are for those who must make their own decisions.

10:37 Two-column tables are best left without any rules (see table 1). In general, all tables of more than two columns should carry vertical rules throughout. It is permissible, however, to omit the rules between columns covered by a spanner heading (see par. 10:16), provided that the columns are not too close together. In table 3 omission of a rule between columns 1 and 2 and between columns 3 and 4 is allowable; but in table 5 the columns of figures are so close together that rules are important for ease of reading, and therefore are not omitted. It is increasingly common to omit all vertical rules, even in very large tables, and this is permissible if columns are appropriately spaced. Such tables are termed "open-style" (see table 6).

TABLE 7—Continued

| United States Civil Cases per Judge (United States a Party) | | | | | | Private Civil Cases per Judge, Total | |
| Total | | OPA | | Other United States | | | |
Florida (Northern)	84 Districts	Florida (Northern)	84 Districts	Florida (Northern)	84 Districts	Florida (Northern)	84 Districts
61	72	. . .	. . .	61	72	34	81
59	83	. . .	. . .	59	83	45	82
70	91	. . .	. . .	70	91	33	77
49	100	. . .	12	49	88	30	58
47	113	7	37	40	76	23	56
70	238	6	160	64	78	28	57
103	251	71	174	32	77	28	70
80	162	30	84	50	78	26	109
63	87	6	20	57	67	22	117

10:38   Each ruled table should have a double rule at the top, above the boxheading, and a single rule at the bottom, or end, of the table. There are no vertical rules at the sides of the table.

10:39   It has been noted that blank space should be left on all sides of a boxheading (see par. 10:16). Never begin a heading on the line immediately below the rule, and never begin a rule on the same line as a heading (thus giving the effect of underlined words).

10:40   A rule should be typed above totals at the feet of columns, across the columns but not extending through the stub (see table 3). Subtotals, grand totals, means, and averages are similarly handled.

10:41   Horizontal rules are usually made with the typewriter; vertical rules by hand (using permanent black ink, preferably india ink). A double rule is typed by turning the knob of the roller just slightly before typing the second line. If the carriage of the typewriter takes the paper the long way, all the rules may be made with the typewriter. But using the typewriter to make the vertical rules requires special care if the columns are only one or two spaces apart.

171

11 Illustrations

11:1   In addition to tables, illustrative materials may consist of graphs (pies, curves, and map graphs), charts showing organization of departments, plans, and so on, diagrams of machines and instruments, maps, photographs, commercial illustrations, and original illustrations. Such illustrations are also called "figures."

11:2   It is not within the scope of this *Manual* to give advice on the inclusion of illustrative materials, or on what type or types to use, or, except in general terms, to give instructions on their presentation. These matters are fully treated in a number of specialized books and manuals.[1] However, some general principles need to be summarized to bring the preparation of illustrative materials for a paper into harmony with that of the text.

POSITION

11:3   Illustrations, especially graphs and charts, should be placed as close as possible to their first references in the text. Like tables, they should be referred to by number so that their exact placement is flexible (see par. 10:4). In some papers there may be sound reasons for grouping all the illustrations, if they are of one type, at the end. (In a printed book, photographs and other illustrations printed on paper different from that of the text are frequently placed together rather than scattered through the text.)

[1]One deserves special mention: Frances W. Zweifel, *A Handbook of Biological Illustration*, Phoenix Books (Chicago: University of Chicago Press, 1961). Although as the title implies, the emphasis is on biological illustrations, the treatment of many of the topics is equally helpful in other fields.

PAGE NUMBERS

11:4 When illustrative materials are included with the text, their pages are numbered consecutively with the textual matter. It is not permissible to give them supplementary numbers (e.g., 45*a*) after the text has been numbered. A folded map or chart is numbered in the center at the top of the exposed fold. A frontispiece, which faces the title page, is numbered with the preliminaries, but the page number does not appear.

11:5 Pages of illustrations placed together at the end of the paper should follow the pagination of the text.

MARGINS

11:6 A margin of at least one inch (more is permissible) should be allowed on all four sides of a page carrying illustrative material. The number of the illustration and its caption or legend—everything but the number of the page—must fall within the margins (for margins when mounting material, see par. 11:25).

NUMBERS AND LEGENDS

11:7 If a paper contains several types of illustrations such as maps, charts, diagrams, and graphs, it is desirable to label them all as figures and number them consecutively, in arabic numerals. If, however, there is a disproportionately large number of one type, or one type which though not greater in number than the others is seen to be of greater importance for the study, that type may be given its own label and numbered in a separate series: Map 1 or Chart 3 or Graph 4. (See sample F, p. 14.)

11:8 Ordinarily a legend follows the number; this may be in the form of a title, or caption:

```
Fig. 2.  Block diagram of Fern Lake
```

But it is frequently in the form of an explanation consisting of a sentence or more (not necessarily grammatically complete sentences) of explanation. Here the first line is indented like a paragraph and the punctuation follows ordinary sentence style:

Fig. 9.   Relationship between number of buds or leaf scars, number of branches subsequently produced, and length of shoots. Small numbers identify multiple observations of same value.

11:9   The legend should be typed to the width of the illustration, except that short legends are centered.

11:10   Two or more illustrations may appear on the same page, each with its number and legend. Also, two or more related illustrations may be placed on the same page, the group as a whole being given a number and a legend, and the individual illustrations being identified by letter alone (a, b, etc.) or by letter and legend. If space is not sufficient below the individual illustrations for both the letter and the legend, each illustration may simply be lettered, and letters and legends either be grouped at the foot of the page or typed on the opposite page. In the latter instance, the page with the legend is turned over so that the reader will see illustration and legend on facing pages (see par. 10:10).

11:11   A wide illustration may be placed broadside on the page, with the top at the binding side. The legend, with its number, should appear below the illustration, so that it reads up the page. The page number is in its normal position. This same arrangement may be used for a group of illustrations.

11:12   Some illustrations—maps in particular—carry printed or hand-lettered headings at the top or the side of the illustration. In such a case only the number of the illustration is centered below it.

11:13   A key, or scale of miles, if included, should preferably be placed in a convenient space beside the illustration rather than below it.

11:14   If the space below an illustration is not sufficient to carry the number and legend and still allow the one-inch margin at the bottom of the page, they may be centered at the right of the illustration. If there is not enough space at the side, number and legend may be typed on the opposite page (see par. 11:10).

PREPARATION

GRAPHS AND CHARTS

11:15   Line graphs and bar charts may be either (1) drawn in india ink on cross-ruled paper of the same, or approximately the same, quality as the paper used for the text; (2) drawn first on cross-ruled paper, traced on the plain bond paper, and the lines inked in; or (3) drawn first and then reproduced by a suitable photographic process. Graph paper is available ruled either in the metric system or in inches and fractions thereof. Also, the paper is made with lines in one of several colors: black, brown, red, green, violet, blue. The choice of color may depend upon whether the drawing is to be photographed and whether it is desired to show the entire grid system. The pale blue lines will not reproduce in the photographic process.

11:16   When fine detail is to be shown in an illustration, it is sometimes advisable, if not necessary, to make the original drawing larger than could be accommodated on $8\frac{1}{2}$-by-11-inch paper. Made to scale, the illustration is then reduced to page size by photography.

PHOTOGRAPHS

11:17   Photographs may be finished either in the $8\frac{1}{2}$-by-11-inch size so as to avoid mounting, or smaller and mounted two or more to a page on the regular typing paper. If photographs are finished full size, the paper should be medium weight, since the heavier weight tends to break in binding. Matte-surface photographs may be preferred to glossy prints, although the latter make sharper illustrations and are therefore a better choice where minute detail must be shown.

11:18   Commercial illustrations usually require mounting. If several copies of these are needed, and are not available, the originals may be reproduced photographically. If the illustrations are in color, however, photographs may not be satisfactory. The inclusion of illustrations in color requires considerable forethought. As a matter of fact, color cannot be used in a thesis or dissertation for a university or college which requires a planographic or microphotographic reproduction of its theses and dissertations. The photographs and photographic reproductions for use in such theses or dissertations should be on glossy paper.

MAPS

11:19 Many kinds of maps are available ready made, and some may serve satisfactorily with no additions except page and figure number and, possibly, a caption. Some may be used as base maps, with crosshatching, outlining of specific areas, spotting, figures or letters superimposed to produce illustrations adequate for the writer's particular purposes. Unless stippling or crosshatching of only a small area is required, handwork should not be attempted. Two commercial products offer satisfactory methods in combination with handwork: (1) drawing in the conventional manner with black waterproof ink on Craftint, a paper with invisible patterns that are brought out by application of a liquid developer to those parts of the drawing where stippling or crosshatching is desired; (2) drawing outlines on the regular typing paper or on a light-weight drawing paper and applying Zip-a-tone to the areas where stippling or crosshatching is desired. Craftint comes in two styles: singletone Craftint offers three patterns of shading, and the doubletone offers four. A thin adhesive paper, Zip-a-tone is available in many different patterns and is made in two styles, with the printing either on the adhesive side or on the upper surface. The first is the simpler to apply. *The use of either Craftint or Zip-a-tone presupposes photographic reproduction for presentation in the paper.*

11:20 Maps often need to be executed entirely by hand. In the fields of geography and geology, where knowledge of maps and map making is so important an objective in the student's training, handmade maps in theses and dissertations, at least, are likely to be a requirement.

HANDWORK

11:21 Legends and keys, as well as any necessary lines, letters, or symbols in the illustrations proper, may be made either with the typewriter or by hand, using black waterproof drawing ink. For hand lettering, the aid of a stencil or a lettering device is recommended to assure clear, even, well-spaced lettering. Since the use of color is not always feasible, various styles of lines must be used in graphs employing two or more curves; and crosshatching, shading with dots and small circles, or similar devices should be used in bar charts. (See par. 11:19.)

MOUNTING

11:22   Illustrations measuring less than 8½-by-11 inches must be mounted on bond typing paper. Dry mounting tissue is the most satisfactory adhesive for the purpose. Properly applied — and correct application is most important — the mounts will remain firm for many years without causing the slightest deterioration of the illustrations. The tissue is available in sheets or in rolls, accompanied by complete directions for its use, and can be purchased from any photographic supply store.

11:23   Although dry mounting tissue is the preferred adhesive for mountings designed to withstand use for many years, some kinds of white casein glue are a reasonably satisfactory substitute, provided that the glue is applied in such a way that buckling does not result. The secret is in using a small enough quantity so that the liquid does not penetrate the body of the typing paper and cause it to stretch and wrinkle. It would be well to experiment a bit before doing the final mountings. For small mounts, apply the glue thinly just within the edges of the mount. In addition, for larger pieces to be mounted, small dabs of glue applied here and there over the surface may be more satisfactory than its application at the edges alone. The adhesive is applied to the material that is to be mounted, not to the paper beneath it.

11:24   The use of rubber cement for mountings, recommended in earlier editions of this *Manual,* is now discouraged.

11:25   Whether the adhesive used is dry mounting tissue or white casein glue, the area of the paper to be covered by the illustration should be indicated before the mounts are placed by drawing a very light pencil line at the top, or placing a dot at each upper corner. The illustration, or the composite of illustrations, should be centered upon the page. "Centering" in this connection assumes a slightly wider margin at the bottom of the sheet than at the top, and a half-inch wider margin at the left than at the right (to compensate for the visual loss due to the binding).

11:26 As each page of mounted material is finished, it should be set aside to dry for a few minutes (follow precisely the directions for drying mountings made with dry mounting tissue) before being placed under a weight for several hours. It is advisable to protect the newly mounted material by putting a piece of plain paper between each two sheets while they are under a weight.

11:27 A word of caution is not out of place to the student who proposes to develop and print his own photographs. The job should not be attempted by an amateur unless all the proper facilities are at hand and, further, unless there is ample time to carry out the successive steps without hurry and to allow for possible accidents.

11:28 It cannot be emphasized too strongly that sufficient time should be set aside for this job of mounting illustrations. Unless he is cautioned beforehand, the inexperienced person is likely to underestimate grossly the time that is required to do this work satisfactorily.

FOLDING

11:29 Illustrations larger than the normal page size may usually be reduced photographically. If reduction is not feasible, as it may not be in the case of large maps, for example, the material may be folded, provided that the institution for which the paper is prepared does not prohibit folding.

11:30 To fold, work first from right to left, making the first crease no more than 7½ inches from the left side of the sheet. If a second fold is necessary, carry the right-hand portion of the sheet back to the right, making the second crease no more than 6½ inches to the left of the first. Additional folds, if required, should be parallel with the first two. If the folding is done as directed, when the large folded sheet is in place, there will be no danger of the folds at the left being caught in the stitching or of those at the right being sheared off in the process of trimming.

11:31   Folding in more than one direction should be avoided, but, if it is not possible to do so, the sheet should first be folded from bottom to top, making the first fold no more than 10 inches from the top of the sheet. When this first fold has been made, unfold the sheet and cut a strip 1 inch wide from the left-hand side of the sheet, starting at the bottom and continuing up to the fold. The removal of this strip is necessary to prevent the free portion of the sheet from being caught in the stitching. The sheet may then be refolded and folded from right to left as directed above.

12 Scientific Papers

12:1 It is difficult to generalize about the format of scientific papers as distinct from other kinds of scholarly papers, not only because practice varies somewhat from field to field, but also because even within the same field variable factors determine style to some extent. In general, however, there are three major differences between format in nonscientific and in scientific papers: (1) organization, (2) handling of references, and (3) use of numerals, symbols, and abbreviations.

12:2 In such mechanical matters as spacing and pagination, and the presentation of tables and other illustrative materials, the scientific paper should conform in general to the style recommended in this *Manual* under the several headings.

ORGANIZATION

12:3 The length of a paper in part governs how it is divided into sections and whether the sections begin on new pages or not. In a short paper the sections do not usually begin on new pages; the text is typed continuously, with subheadings marking the sections. In longer papers the major sections may or may not be designated as chapters or parts, but usually each begins on a new page.

12:4 In shorter papers the major divisions may or may not be both numbered and titled, but they should be marked by either number or title. In all papers subheadings usually appear within major divisions, but, in general, these should not begin new pages. (Suitable styles of subheadings and some suggestions on their logical order are discussed in par. 1:18.)

12:5   In short papers it is not necessary to include a table of contents, a list of tables, or a list of illustrations, although individual preferences or the demands of a specific piece of writing may call for one or all of these.

LIST OF REFERENCES

12:6   In papers in scientific fields, the general practice is to collect all the references at the end of the paper under some such heading as "List of References" or "Literature Cited." The term "Bibliography" appears less often, since for the most part it is not appropriate, the "List" usually being confined to those works mentioned in the paper. But if the list actually is a bibliography, it should be so headed.

12:7   Under the list scheme — regardless of its heading — footnotes are usually *not* employed to give sources. Instead, short references to items in the list appear in the text itself. There are two commonly used styles for this (see pars. 12:8, 12:12), the first of which is usually preferred.

12:8   Under the first scheme the text reference gives, in parentheses, the surname of the author with year date of the publication; or year date alone if the author's name occurs in the sentence:

```
These results were later confirmed (Naismith 1971).
Naismith (1971) was able to confirm these results.
```

12:9   The list of references at the end of the paper is arranged alphabetically by authors' surnames. Two or more works by the same author are listed chronologically, by date of publication. Two or more works by the same author published in the same year are identified as, for example, 1964*a*, 1964*b*. In a succession of works by the same author, the name is given for the first entry, and an eight-space line (i.e., the underlining key struck eight times) ending with a period replaces it in succeeding entries (see par. 7:24). If a title edited by the author follows immediately one of which he is the author, an eight-space line ending with a comma and followed by "ed." is used, but if the name is followed by a title of which he is coauthor, his name should be repeated in full, followed by the names of his coauthors (see par. 7:9). Unless a particular purpose is served by numbering the entries in the list, numbering is omitted. Suggested styles of entries are the following:

Article

```
Mohr, H. 1962. Primary effect of light on growth.
    Ann. Rev. Plant Physiol. 13:465-88. [Note
    that capitalization of the title of the article
    should be that used in a sentence.]
```

Book

```
Kramer, P. J., and Kozlowski, T. T. 1960. Physiology
    of trees, p. 11. New York: McGraw-Hill.
    ["Sentence" capitalization for book title.]
```

12:10 If reference to specific parts of a work—page(s), table, illustration—is desired, the notation should be included in the textual reference rather than in the entry in the list:

```
Analysis of the paired-data variance (Goulden 1952,
table 2) yields . . .
```

```
Ulrich (1927, p. 29 and fig. 2) divided the
pairs . . .
```

12:11 In the examples of entries in a list of references (see par. 12:9), the reference to a journal article cites the title of the article, using capitalization as in a sentence. In some fields it is usual to omit the title of the article. The decision to include or to omit the titles must be made before the list is compiled, and one scheme followed consistently. The student may be guided in this decision by observing the general practice of journals in his field. If the paper is to be submitted to a specific journal for publication, it is well to follow exactly the style of reference used by that journal.

12:12 The second style of reference places a number after the the author's name in the text, enclosing the number either in parentheses or in square brackets [ ]:

```
Whitehead [5] spoke of "nature alive" and "nature
lifeless" . . .
```

```
Numerous studies (21-35) have been published
in which . . .
```

12:13   The items in the list are then numbered in sequence according to the first mention of each in the text. Subsequent references to a work use the same number. This scheme has the obvious disadvantage that it cannot be in alphabetical order and that, once it is compiled and numbers assigned to each entry, no additional reference may be inserted in the text without renumbering all following items in the list; use of numbers such as 4*a* is not permitted. The scheme of reference described in paragraph 12:8, which is far less susceptible to error than that of paragraph 12:12, is therefore to be preferred.

12:14   Under either scheme, standard abbreviations for the names of journals are recommended. The writer should consult a list of abbreviations commonly used in his particular field. These lists are often published by a leading journal in the field. If the names of publishers of books are given in shortened form, as is recommended, standard abbreviations should be used in accordance with the list given in *Books in Print*, published annually by R. R. Bowker Co., New York, or, for British publishers, in *British Books in Print: The Reference Catalogue of Current Literature*, published by J. Whitaker & Sons, London.

FOOTNOTES

12:15   Although the practice of collecting references in a list at the end of the paper appears to be growing in use, it is by no means uniform even within a given field, and the use of footnotes for citing references is not uncommon. The style of footnote entry used in chemistry is shown in paragraph 12:20; that in physics, in paragraph 12:22. If you do not know the style to use in your paper, you should consult the particular style manual or guide prepared by the outstanding scholarly association in your field. Titles of some of these are given at the end of the Preface of this *Manual*.

12:16   Relevant material not of sufficient importance to be brought into the text of the paper should be handled as a footnote. When the scheme adopted is to put references to the literature into footnotes, content footnotes should be numbered consecutively with the reference footnotes. When, however, the scheme is to put references to the literature into a list at the end of the paper, relevant remarks should not be incorporated into that list, but set as footnotes marked by an asterisk (*). If there is more than one note on a page, the second is marked by double asterisks (**), the third by triple asterisks (***). (See par. 10:35 for additional symbols. Do not use more than three asterisks.)

STYLES OF REFERENCE

12:17 The following examples are for entries in a list of references in some cases and for footnotes in others. They are patterned after the styles used by the leading publications in the several fields.

ANTHROPOLOGY

12:18 There is some variation in practice within this field. The scheme of the *American Anthropologist* is shown here. References to the literature are given in the text of the paper. The author's surname (unless it occurs in the text), year date of the publication, and page number are enclosed in parentheses: "(Herskovits 1952: 12)." An alphabetized bibliography at the end of the paper supplies complete information in the following forms:

Journal reference

KLUCKHOHN, C.
1943   Covert culture and administrative
                problems. American Anthropologist
                45: 213–27.

Book reference

SCHALLER, G. B.
1963   The mountain gorilla. Chicago,
                University of Chicago Press.

PHYSIOLOGY

12:19 Uses a list of references alphabetically arranged. Note the omission of underlining.

Journal reference

Hildebrandt, A. C. 1948. Influence of some carbon compounds on growth of brain tissues in vitro. Anat. Record 100:674.

Book reference

Schwarts, R. J. 1955. The complete dictionary of abbreviations. T. Y. Crowell Co., New York.

PSYCHOLOGY

Uses a list of references arranged alphabetically:

Journal reference

Archer, P. W. The tactile perception of roughness. American Journal of Psychology, 1950, 63, 365–373.

Book reference

Jackson, J. W. The psychology of industrial unrest. New York: McGraw-Hill, 1948.

CHEMISTRY

12:20   Uses footnote references, each bearing a number:

Journal reference

(10) W. G. Lloyd and C. E. Lange, J. Am. Chem. Soc., 86, 1491 (1964).

Book reference

(18) J. S. Rowlinson, "Liquids and Liquid Mixtures," Butterworth, London. 1959, p. 14.

MATHEMATICS

12:21   Uses an alphabetized list of references, each entry being numbered:

Journal reference

7.   Hans Samelson, Topology of Lie groups, Bull. Amer. Math. Soc. 58 (1952), 2–37.

Book reference

9.   G. N. Watson, A treatise on the theory of Bessel
        functions, 2d ed., Cambridge, 1962, p. 11.

PHYSICS

12:22   Uses footnote references:

Journal reference

[1]P. G. Burke and K. Smith, Rev. Mod. Phys. 34,
458 (1962).

Book reference

[4]H. A. Bethe, Intermediate Quantum Mechanics
(Benjamin, New York, 1964), pp. 29–30.

NUMERALS, SYMBOLS, AND ABBREVIATIONS

12:23   The demand in scientific papers for the use of numbers
and units of measurement expressed in numerical values
makes it suitable for purposes of clarity to use figures,
symbols, and abbreviations to an extent not considered
good form in nonscientific writing. Aside from a few rules
here set down (pars. 12:24–27), the writer must settle on
the scheme he will use—preferably when working on his
first draft—and maintain the same usage throughout the
paper.

12:24   Spell out a number at the beginning of a sentence, even if
it is part of a connected group in which numerals are used
after it. A better plan in such a case is to reconstruct the
sentence so that it does not begin with a number.

12:25   Spell out expressions of measurement when they are not
preceded by numbers.

12:26   To avoid confusion, you may spell out one set of figures in
an expression that involves two or more series of figures:

In a test given six months later, ninety–seven
children made no errors; eighty–two made 1–2 errors;
sixty–four made 3–4 errors.

12:27   Do not use the symbol for *percent* (%) when it is not pre-ceded by a figure. And note that *percentage*, not *percent* or %, is the correct expression to use when no figure is given:

> The September scores showed an improvement of 70.1%
> [or 70.1 percent if the writer prefers the word to
> the symbol]. Thus the percentage of achievers in the
> second test indicated . . .

12:28   In mathematical text the demands for the use of symbols and abbreviations are so complicated, and vary so much from one paper to another, that no suggestions can be given here. Students in this field should receive training in correct usage along with their education in the science. Editors of some of the mathematical periodicals have pre-pared manuals for authors which give useful suggestions.

13 Typing the Paper

RESPONSIBILITY OF WRITER AND OF TYPIST

13:1 The writer is responsible for the correct presentation of his paper in its entirety—all the preliminary, illustrative, and reference matter as well as the main body of the text. Beyond the production of an accurate transcription of the copy, the typist should be held responsible only for mechanical details having to do with spacing, neatness, and the general appearance of the final copy.

13:2 Although this chapter is designed especially to guide the typist, it does not contain all that he or she needs to know in order to produce a paper in acceptable final form. Familiarity with the greater part of this *Manual* is necessary. Some rules for dividing words at ends of lines are given in chapter 3 (pars. 3:35–51). Two chapters, "Tables" and "Illustrations," require the typist's close attention, since the nature and complexity of illustrative materials demand that the writer of the paper be given virtually the same information for the preparation of his original copy as that needed by the typist who sets up the final copy. To avoid duplication, that information is not repeated in this chapter on typing.

TYPEWRITER

13:3 Either pica or elite type, or one of the types available on some of the newer typewriter models, is satisfactory for most typing jobs, although some institutions specify pica type for theses and dissertations. A typist who expects to do any considerable amount of typing of theses, dissertations, or other formal papers – particularly those designed for submission to publishers – would do well to be prepared with a specially equipped typewriter, preferably with pica type. The special vertical spacing obtainable with the five-line ratchet is recommended for the typing of copy that is to be reproduced by offset lithography (such as Multilith or Planograph), and it may be used for any other copy, subject to the approval of the person for whom the copy is to be prepared. The same ratchet permits single and double spacing, and the accurate half-space turn of the roller is a great convenience in the typing of superscripts and subscripts. Keys with the grave accent mark (`), the acute accent mark (´), the circumflex (^), the plus symbol (+), the plus-and-minus symbol (±), and the square brackets ([ ]) are almost indispensable. For the correct expression of the more common foreign accent marks, see chapter 4, par. 4:34. Some of the symbols carried on the standard keyboard are used less frequently in the typing of formal papers than in commercial work and can be replaced with the more necessary symbols at a nominal charge. Some typewriters now available have certain keys that are designed for easy removal and replacement with others. The manufacturers stock a wide variety of characters and will make others to order at reasonable prices.

13:4   Both type and rollers should be kept clean by the use of a specially treated paper. After placing the typewriter in stencil position, the special paper is inserted and each key is struck firmly five or six times, or until the impression leaves no ink smudge. The rollers are cleaned during the typing operation. Periodically, a thorough check of the typewriter should be made by a responsible serviceman to insure smooth rollers, uniformity of letter impression, alignment of letters, and proper adjustment of tension.

RIBBON

13:5   Ribbons of superior quality are most satisfactory in the long run. Medium-inked black ribbons produce greater uniformity of impression than the light-inked or the heavy-inked. To secure superior uniformity of type color, it is

189

desirable to have on hand before the typing is begun enough ribbons of the same kind to complete the job, and to rotate them at regular intervals, of, say, every twenty-five pages. This is particularly desirable in typing copy for offset lithography. On some electric machines, use of a one-time carbon ribbon produces copy of extremely high quality.

PAPER

13:6 A good grade of bond paper should be used. Do not use one of the so-called erasable papers, unless it is specified by the institution to which the paper is to be presented. Some institutions have specific requirements for theses and dissertations. If there are no such requirements, paper of 20-pound weight and at least 50 percent rag content should be used. Some institutions permit a lighter weight, or even machine copies, for the carbon copies.

CARBON PAPER

13:7 The carbon paper should be of good quality: black, hard finish (nongreasy), light- or medium-weight (light-weight is preferable if several copies are to be made). Such carbon paper makes a gray rather than a black impression, but the letters are sharper, and the copies smudge less and remain in good condition longer than those made with paper of a soft or medium finish.

13:8 The use of carbon paper on which the lines are numbered in a vertical column visible at the right of the typing paper is preferred by some typists to the guide sheet mentioned below (see par. 13:28).

CORRECTIONS AND ERASURES

13:9 No interlineations, crossing out of letters or words, strike-overs, or *extensive* erasures are permissible. A correction fluid, Liquid Paper, when properly applied, is satisfactory for making corrections.

13:10 Deletion or addition of more than one letter after the line has been completed should be made by retyping. By skillful use of the back-spacer, the letters of a word can be crowded so that the space normally occupied by a word of given length can be made to accommodate a word having one more letter. This must be done by erasing the entire word and reducing evenly the space between the letters, not by crowding just two letters. Extensive correction of a page once passed calls for great care in retyping so that the material may be equalized and the last line on the page properly spaced out to the end. Erasures should be reduced to a minimum and made with such skill on both the original and the copies that they will not be noticeable. Wherever possible they should be made before the page is removed from the typewriter. Typists should form the habit of looking over each page before removing it from the machine. Once withdrawn, each copy of the set should be corrected separately by direct type rather than all together by restacking and insertion of carbons. Care should be taken to strike the keys heavily or lightly, as the case may require, so that the corrected portions may match in color as nearly as possible the remainder of the typed material upon the page.

13:11 An erasing shield and two ink erasers — one with a broad edge for covering larger areas and one with a narrow edge for the smaller ones — are indispensable. To prevent smudging of the face copy, the fingers should rest on the erasing shield. To prevent smudging of the carbon copies, a piece of paper should be placed between each sheet of carbon and the page beneath.

13:12 Corrections on copy prepared for offset lithography must not be made by erasing. Liquid Paper may be used, or a chemically treated paper such as KO-REC-TYPE (for the face copy) and KO-REC-COPY (for carbon copy) which will remove mistakes in typing both on the original and the carbon copy (or copies) in one easy operation. If errors on copy for offset lithography are not corrected in that way, the corrected word or words should be retyped on a separate piece of paper and placed over the errors, attaching with a light coating of white casein glue (see par. 11:23). Great care must be taken to place the patch accurately and neatly and to leave no dark lines or specks

191

which would show in the printed copy. Typing the corrections on white gummed paper is an alternative to typing on plain paper and pasting.

TYPING THE FRONT MATTER

TITLE PAGE

13:13   See paragraph 1:3 and example of title page (p. 3).

TABLE OF CONTENTS

13:14   The writer of the paper is responsible for the content and style of the table of contents (see pars. 1:4–11). The samples shown in chapter 1 (pp. 11–13) illustrate four styles of tables of contents. Matters of spacing and alignment to be observed by the typist are:

The heading TABLE OF CONTENTS (or CONTENTS) is centered on the twelfth line from the top of the page.

If the paper is divided into PARTS, the part number and title is centered above the chapters they include (samples A and C).

Vertical spacing is as follows: *Triple* between TABLE OF CONTENTS (or CONTENTS) and first entry, and between PART and preceding entry. *Double* between PART and the following entry, between chapter headings, and between chapter headings and the first entry of a subheading. *Single* between individual subheadings. (See samples A and B.)

A heading of such length that it would extend beyond the point of the last period leader is divided and the runover is aligned vertically with the preceding line (see samples A and B). For the heading of a part, however, which is centered upon the page, the runover is also centered (sample A). And for a subheading, the runover is indented three spaces.

Chapter headings begin on the third space after the period following the chapter number, or of the last numeral of the chapter number if there is no period.

Chapter numbers when expressed in numerals are so aligned vertically that the longest number begins at the margin (samples A, B, and C). If the numbers are spelled out, the longest *word* begins at the margin. Thus if there are periods following the numbers (these are optional), the periods will be aligned vertically:

```
     I.                One.
    II.      or        Two.
   III.                Three.
```

Period leaders must always be aligned vertically, and there should be at least three to four spaces between the last period and the first digit of the longest page number. Page numbers are aligned vertically so that the last digit is next to the right-hand margin.

13:15   If a table of contents including both chapter headings and subheadings must be continued to a second page (or more), so apportion the material that if possible a major heading and all its subheadings appear on the same page. An exception may be made when a complete chapter unit is long, but in no case should a major heading be placed at the foot of a page with fewer than two lines of subheading (two lines, not necessarily two subheadings) beneath it. Begin a continuation on the sixth line from the top of the page and omit any heading (such as, TABLE OF CONTENTS – CONTINUED or CONTINUED).

13:16   If a table of contents occupies less than a page, the entire body of material should be approximately centered vertically upon the page. (See par. 11:25 for an interpretation of centering.) The heading, however, should never be set higher than the twelfth line from the top of the page, and the space between the final line of typing and the bottom of the sheet should never be less than one inch.

LIST OF ILLUSTRATIONS

13:17   The writer of the paper is responsible for providing copy for the list of illustrations (which may be headed simply Illustrations). If in addition to figures, the list includes another designation such as "maps" or "charts" or "diagrams," and the list so designated is not too long to be accommodated on the same page with the list of figures, that list may either precede or follow the list of figures, depending upon its length. (See pars. 1:11–12 and sample F.) The heading should appear on the twelfth line from the top of the page, or lower if the list is short (see par. 11:25). Period leaders connect the individual legends with page numbers.

LIST OF TABLES

13:18   As reference to the sample lists in chapter 1 (pp. 14–15) will show, the list of tables is similar in style to the list of illustrations. (See par. 1:13 and sample G.) The heading, which may be Tables, omitting the words "List of," is typed on the twelfth line from the top of the page, or farther down if the list is short (see par. 11:25).

TYPING THE TEXT

MARGINS

13:19   Leave a margin of at least one inch on each of the four sides of the sheet. Some institutions require more than this, particularly on the left, since binding reduces the margin. On the first page of every major division of the paper (see par. 13:23), leave two inches at the top above the heading (i.e., begin typing on the twelfth line from the top).

INDENTION

13:20   Indent paragraphs six to eight spaces, unless other specific regulations are made. Follow the same scheme of paragraph indention consistently.

SPACING

13:21   The text should be typed either double space, one and one-half space, or a spacing provided on some of the newer typewriters that is somewhere between one and one-half and double space.

13:22   Leave one space after commas and semicolons, and after colons except in scriptural references, between hours and minutes, and between volume and page numbers (Rom. 8:14–20, 4:30 P.M., 3:25–26), and except in such instances as in paragraphs 2:5, 3:42, 3:47, where more spaces may follow the colon. Leave two spaces after punctuation ending sentences. Do not space after periods in such abbreviations as i.e., e.g., A.M., P.M. (or a.m., p.m.), A.D., B.C., U.S., N.Y., B.A., Ph.D.; but leave a space after periods following initials of personal names, as J. R. C. Stewart. Distinguish between a hyphen and a dash, which on a typewriter is made with two close-spaced hyphens. Leave no space before or after hyphens or dashes:

```
Midland is a fast-growing city.
```

```
The scheme proposed may--in fact, does--meet all the
stated requirements.
```

MAJOR HEADINGS

13:23   Begin every major division (i.e., contents, preface, list of tables, list of illustrations, introduction, each new chapter, bibliography, appendix) on a new page. Center the heading in capital letters on the twelfth line from the top of the sheet. If the paper is divided into sections termed "chapters," the chapter number appears alone (e.g., "CHAPTER I") on the twelfth line, and the chapter title is centered on the third line beneath it. If the word *chapter* is not formally expressed and the sections are merely numbered, the number and title (e.g., "I. THE WORLD OF 1815") are centered on the twelfth line. If the title is longer than 48 spaces, set it in two (or more) double-spaced lines, in inverted-pyramid form. Use no punctuation at the ends of lines. Begin typing the text or the first entry of a list (contents, etc.), on the third line below the heading.

SUBHEADINGS

13:24   (For capitalization and style of subheadings see pars. 1:18–19.) A centered subheading of more than 48 spaces should be divided into two or more single-spaced lines, in inverted-pyramid form. A side heading of more than a half-line should be divided more or less evenly into two (or more) single-spaced lines, the runovers beginning at the margin. Paragraph headings should be underlined and should end with a period. All other subheadings should omit punctua- at the ends of lines.

13:25 All subheadings begin on the third line below text. If two (or more) subheadings appear together (i.e., without intervening text), a double space (blank line) should be left between them, and a double space left also between the subheading and the text following.

TYPING THE FOOTNOTES

SPACING, INDENTION, FOOTNOTE NUMERAL

13:26 Separate text and footnotes with an unbroken line twenty spaces in length, beginning at the left-hand margin on the first line beneath the text. The first line of footnote material is on the second line below this (the third line under the text). Indent the first line of each footnote the same number of spaces as the paragraph indention in the text. Type the footnotes single space, but use double space between individual notes.

13:27 Place the footnote numeral slightly above the line (never a full space above). There should be no punctuation after the numeral and no extra space between it and the first word of the note:

[1]Gabriel Marcel, The Mystery of Being, 1:42.

Since most typewriters lack the numeral one, the small "ell"—l—is used in its place, in footnotes and elsewhere. The capital "eye"—I—should be used only for the roman numeral one, never for the arabic 1.

ESTIMATING SPACE FOR TEXT AND FOOTNOTES

13:28 To place the footnotes correctly on the page and maintain the proper margin at the foot of the page, a *guide sheet* should be used. A special carbon paper may be used (see 13:8) or a sheet may be made of firm, light-weight wrapping paper. Cut it the same length as the typing paper and one-half inch wider. Measure off top and bottom margins to correspond with those used on the typed page, insert the paper into the typewriter, and, beginning with "1" on the line with that occupied by the first line of text on the typed page, number down the extreme right-hand edge of the guide sheet to the line opposite that of the last line of typed matter. It is helpful also to indicate in the top and bottom margins of the guide sheet the point opposite which the page number should appear (see pars. 13:38–41).

13:29   Before rolling the paper and guide sheet into the typewriter, place the guide sheet beneath the bottom sheet of typing paper; align the top and left-hand edges of paper, carbon paper, and guide sheet so that the numbered edge of the guide sheet extends beyond the typing paper; and roll the stacked paper into the typewriter. It may be necessary to adjust the top edges after the paper is placed in the machine.

13:30   When the first footnote number appears in the text, stop and count the number of lines in the corresponding footnote, add two to allow for the line of separation, and deduct this total from the total number of type lines as shown on the guide sheet. The difference between the two figures will give the number of the line at the end of which to stop typing text in order to allow proper space for the footnote. As each succeeding footnote number appears in the text, add the number of lines in the corresponding footnote, allowing one extra for the space between notes, and again determine the number of text lines to be typed.

13:31   All will go according to plan, and the bottom margin will be the proper depth unless a footnote number occurs in the last line of text after all available footnote space has been allotted. Make it a habit to look ahead so as to discover such a difficulty in advance, and avoid the necessity of retyping the page by omitting the last line, even though this will result in a bottom margin deeper than usual.

CONTINUATION OF A LONG FOOTNOTE

13:32   A similar difficulty arises when a footnote number shows the corresponding footnote to be longer than can be accommodated in the space remaining on the page. This calls for a division of the footnote.

13:33   Begin the note on the page where reference to it appears in the text and type as much as the page will allow, taking care to break the note within a sentence. Carry the remainder into the footnote area of the next page, where it precedes the footnotes for that page. To indicate the continuation of a footnote by such a statement as "Continued on the next page" is bad form.

ARRANGEMENT OF SHORT FOOTNOTES

13:34   To avoid the unattractive appearance and the waste of space which result from the placement of many short footnotes, each on a line by itself and separated from its fellows by extra space above and below, it is advisable to let such short notes follow each other on the same line. There must, however, be at least three spaces between notes, and *all the notes on one line must be complete*:

> [1]Kirk, <u>Keats</u>, p. 37.   [2]Ibid., p. 42.   [3]Ibid.

It is not permissible to carry over to the next line a part of the last note. Similarly, it is not permissible to utilize the blank space following a note of more than one line in length to insert a short note.

<u>Wrong</u>:   [1]Duff, <u>Literary History of Rome</u>, p. 2. [2]Ibid., p. 180.

<u>Right</u>:   [1]Duff, <u>Literary History of Rome</u>, p. 2. [2]Ibid., p. 180.

<u>Wrong</u>:   [1]Gabriel Marcel, <u>The Mystery of Being</u>, 2 vols. (Chicago: Henry Regnery Co., 1960).   [2]Ibid., 1:6.

<u>Right</u>:   [1]Gabriel Marcel, <u>The Mystery of Being</u>, 2 vols. (Chicago: Henry Regnery Co., 1960). [2]Ibid., 1:6.

ARRANGEMENT OF FOOTNOTES ON A SHORT PAGE

13:35   When the final material of a chapter is contained on part of of a page, any footnotes applicable to the page should be arranged in the usual style after the space and separating line, immediately below the text.

ARRANGEMENT OF FOOTNOTES IN A QUOTATION

13:36   When a single-spaced, indented quotation includes one or more reference indexes from the source being quoted, the corresponding footnotes should be placed beneath the quotation, separated from the last line of the quotation by an eight-space rule (i.e., striking the key for underlining eight times). The reference indexes and the footnotes should follow exactly the form used in the original (see par. 6:11). References added by the writer of the paper should be numbered in sequence with the paper's notes and the footnotes placed at the bottom of the page.

TYPING THE REFERENCE MATTER

13:37   (For typing appendixes, glossary, and list of abbreviations, see pars. 1:24–26.) In a bibliography, entries may be typed single space, double space, or one and one-half space. If single spacing is used, there should be a double space between entries. Each item should begin at the left margin and succeeding lines should be indented a definite number of spaces. (In the sample entries shown in chapter 8, the indention is six spaces, i.e., typing begins at the seventh space.) If desired, the authors' names may be typed in capitals throughout. Annotations should begin a new line and should be typed single space (see par. 7:33).

PAGINATION

13:38   Assign a number to every page of the paper except the blank sheet following the title page. On the title page—and the part-title pages, if there are any—the numbers are not shown, but the pages are counted in the pagination.

13:39   For the preliminaries, number with small roman numerals (ii, iii, iv, etc.) centered at the bottom of the page on the fifth line above the edge. The numbering begins with "ii"; the title page counts as page i, unless there is a frontispiece, which becomes page i, the title page ii. These numbers do not appear, that is, they should not be typed on the pages.

13:40   Number the remaining parts, including text, illustrations, appendix, and bibliography with arabic numerals, centered at the top of the page on the fifth line below the edge, except that on every page with a major heading (e.g., the first page of a chapter, of the bibliography, etc.), place the number at the foot of the page, centered on the fifth line above the edge. Begin the numbering of the main body of the paper with "1" and run consecutively to the end.

13:41   An alternate scheme of pagination is that of numbering all pages in the upper right-hand corner—excepting of course the title page and part-title pages.

SAMPLE TYPESCRIPT

13:42   The following two pages reproduce a typescript showing the opening pages of a chapter.[1] The text is double spaced; the block quotations and the footnotes are single spaced. The paragraph indention is eight spaces. The block quotations are indented four spaces in their entirety; if one quotation had begun with a paragraph, the paragraph indention would have been another four spaces.

[1]The sample pages are taken from a 1954 Ph.D. dissertation by St. Clair Drake, "Value Systems, Social Structure, and Race Relations in the British Isles" (University of Chicago) and are reproduced here with the kind permission of the author. Footnote style of the original has been altered to follow current practice.

CHAPTER II   *12th line*

THE DEVELOPMENT OF A RACE RELATIONS   *15th line*

ACTION-STRUCTURE   *17th line*

Race Relations in the British   *20th line*
Isles: 1700 to the First   *21st line*
World War   *22d line*

From the defeat of the Spanish Armada in 1588 until the abolition *24th l.*
of slavery throughout the British Empire in 1833, the economy of Britain
was tied, in some measure, to the fortunes of the African slave trade. In
the colonies of the West Indies and the southern United States, and later in
South Africa, black plantation labor produced wealth that flowed home to
Britain. In Britain itself, slave labor did not take root, although retired
planters and a rising commercial middle class sometimes used slaves as
servants. A small Negro population was living in London by 1700, and some
sources have estimated that by 1770 there were between 14,000 and 20,000
Negroes residing in greater London out of a total population of some
123,000.[1]   They were mainly slaves and domestic servants living in white

45th l.
47th l.

[1]This would be about the same percentage as Negroes constitute of
the present Chicago population. Little cites these estimates (Kenneth L.
Little, Negroes in Britain: A Study of Racial Relations in English Society
[London: Kegan Paul, Trench, Truebner & Co., 1947], p. 170), but notes that
C. M. MacInnes, in England and Slavery (London: J. W. Arrowsmith, 1934),
"doubts if the total slave population in England ever rose above 15,000 or
at most 20,000." One of the leading authorities on the social history of
the period, M. Dorothy George, puts the number of Negro slaves at "between
14,000 and 15,000." She states that "a large proportion of these must have
been in London, where they seem to have lived chiefly in the eastern and
riverside parishes." (See M. Dorothy George, London Life in the XVIIIth

69

homes, and of their relations with whites of their own class, one student 7th line

has written:

> . . . colour sensibility as such was very little in evidence. . . .
> No doubt Negroes in general were thought of more as slaves and servants
> than anything else, but there appears to have been no aversion to meeting
> or mixing with a person simply on the ground of his colour. [1]

During this same period there were about 10,000 Irish and 20,000 Jews in

London. Hostility toward them was great, and one student has said:

> All foreigners in London who had an outlandish look were likely to be
> roughly treated, or at least abused, by the mob. Jews were very
> unpopular. . . . Jew-baiting became a sport, like cock-throwing or bull-
> baiting, or pelting some poor wretch in the pillory. [2]

There were individuals among both the adherents of Conservative and

Liberal-humanitarian ideological systems who felt that, even though slavery

flourished in the colonies, it should not be permitted on British soil.

There were others who felt that the slave trade, if not slavery itself,

should be abolished. One zealous figure, Granville Sharp, through a series

of court cases, was able to have slavery on British soil declared illegal,

by judicial act, in 1772. But the Negro population referred to above con-

tinued to persist, and even to increase. Negro slaves from the West Indies

often attempted to jump ship and claim freedom because they were on British

soil. Of these individuals who were claiming sanctuary, one magistrate wrote:

> . . . they [slaves] no sooner arrive here than they put themselves on a
> footing with other servants, become intoxicated with liberty, grow
> refractory, and either by persuasion of others, or from their own
> inclinations, begin to expect wages according to their own opinion of
> their merits. [3]

Century [New York: Alfred A. Knopf, 1926], p. 131.)

[1] Little, Negroes in Britain, p. 203.

[2] George, London Life in the XVIIIth Century, p. 132.

[3] Little, Negroes in Britain, p. 176.

Index

Index

Index

Index

Index